SHA

SHATTERED DREAMS

An Abused Wife's Escape to Freedom

Susan Stewart

MAINSTREAM
PUBLISHING

EDINBURGH AND LONDON

First published in Great Britain in 1998 by
MAINSTREAM PUBLISHING COMPANY (EDINBURGH) LTD
7 Albany Street
Edinburgh EH1 3UG

ISBN 1 85158 990 2

A catalogue record for this book is available from the British Library

Typeset in 10 on 11pt Janson Text
Printed and bound in Finland by WSOY

This book is dedicated to my three beautiful bairns with all my love

ACKNOWLEDGEMENTS

I must thank Drew McAdam for his help and encouragement in my writing. He was the only person ever to do so, and for that I remain grateful. I also thank Pat Tilson for her powers of inspiration, and Graham Tilson for his practical assistance.

The efforts of the Woman's Aid branch which gave me and my family refuge in 1995 are much appreciated – all those involved will know who they are. Despite the unfortunate incident that occurred during my time there, I would continue to urge any woman who suffers abuse within a relationship to approach this organisation without hesitation.

And finally, thank you Mum. Without your help, love and support this book would not have been written.

CHAPTER ONE

The door slammed, the house was empty. 'Bastard!' Then the car started up, clicked through the gears and pulled away. 'Fat, ugly bastard that he is!' It was a beautiful day – weatherwise anyway, and blissfully quiet.

'Rip his bloody fat head off . . .'

There were no neighbours milling about, no curtains twitching. When Marjery phoned she seemed relieved to hear my voice. 'Suzy? Was it you that phoned? God, what happened?'

'Well, it was Sam that called you . . .'

'We didn't know what it was, I mean the noise! Was it him? I knew there was somethin' wrong wi' him yesterday . . . what happened then?' She wheezed an agitated silence.

'Och, Sam just thought he'd give you a wee call to let you hear him kicking me around the living-room.'

'Oh . . .'

'Aye. The noise was a joint affair with Ryan, David and me all screaming for him to stop hitting me. Oh, and the banging noises? That would be when he was hitting me across the head with the receiver, but when the cord wouldn't stretch far enough he dropped that and just punched me with his fist.'

'Oh right.'

'Of course his greatest achievement I thought, was that he did all that with Rosie sitting on his left hip without catching her even once – you know, with a stray slap or something. If you had seen it, instead of just listening, I'm sure you'd have been impressed Marjery.' Now I was getting sarcastic, not that she noticed.

'Well . . . well that's terrible. He shouldn't do that in front of the bairns, I mean, that's terrible.' She stuttered.

'He shouldn't do it at all Marjery!'

'No, no, well, where is he? I'll talk to him, you tell him. I mean we just answer the phone an' we hear screamin' and crying. ' thought "this has tae be a wrong number!" We never thought it was Sam. I mean, why us, Christ? I mean, it's no' a very nice way to start yer Sunday . . . well is it?'

In the space of three minutes, Marjery Brown had turned the entire incident around, so that it was she who was the object of his anger. As if she needed a reason to talk to him; like him punching her daughter- in-law around the house of a Sunday morning just didn't warrant a telling off.

At least she had heard it I thought, as I eased myself back into the garden chair. The sun had warmed it tenderly for me in my absence. Then, as usual, the memory had rewound and was playing itself back to me, without my consent. Every detail. His face, twisted with hate. Even the beads of sweat dotted around his temples, I could see it all. And the children, God the poor wee souls. With their strained faces and darting eyes, taking it all in. All the terror locked inside their heads. And the noise, the bloody noise . . .

I let the image run to it's merciless finale, while my heart tap-danced vindictively within me. I slowly raised a hand to smooth my neck (what a place to punch someone!) and my jaw and the side of my head. The size of his fist meant that my ear had received a knuckle or two, and it still throbbed. Then my back, well there really wasn't anything else left to punch since I was on my knees with my hands around my head. Must be a natural reaction that.

Millions of battle-wearied soldiers will have attempted to protect themselves from devastating explosions in the same manner no doubt. I wondered if they had been as frightened as I was. Did they feel as humiliated? Probably not, since there was no point in them taking it personally. That was always my failing, Sam would say. He never actually meant to frighten me or humiliate me in any way. He always made a point of assuring me of that.

I pressed my bare feet onto the warm concrete, lifting my face to the sky with eyes closed and began to day dream. I amused myself with images of Sam entering the house, the kids would be somewhere else, enjoying themselves, and it would just be him and me. I am smiling, happy to see him and I take his large sweaty hand and gently lead him out into the garden where he sees his entire family standing. They are relaxed and seemingly happy, smiling graciously while lifting delicate champagne glasses in acknowledgement. He nods and waves to them before accepting a slender glass which I pass to him and he begins to relax, but not completely. He sips his champagne politely and very quietly. His eyes dart everywhere, taking in every detail, while his mind assesses the situation, much like I do just before one of his explosions.

Somebody's dog sniffs his trouser leg, and then positions itself agilely before emptying its bladder over his shoe. He looks down horrified, but he doesn't make a scene or hop about complaining loudly. Something I could never do either. Instead, he restrains himself from kicking the animal, and glances at me, forcing a false smile. And then, amidst the gentle tinkling of slender glasses and the soothing murmur of good conversation in the background, and the beautiful day before us, then it would happen. I attempt to glide effortlessly across the lawn towards somebody, and I happen to trip over the cable of the lawnmower. I flail about clumsily, but nobody takes much notice and nobody laughs.

Suddenly, the once serene atmosphere is filled with the most obscene language, and all heads turn round to the source. It's me, rigid with rage.

'What the fuck is this bloody lawnmower doin' here?' I roar as I kick viciously at the cable. 'Just lying here, like it doesn't have a fuckin' garage to go to, I mean you just can't move for all the rubbish lyin' around this fuckin' tip!' I throw my glass at the family, who stand motionless and unaffected by my tantrum. No one answers me, they just stand and stare.

Sam turns to me, his hands outstretched. His palms are raised to the sun, and he tells me to calm down, that it's only a lawn mower cable, that he'll put it away immediately. He tries to explain why it is still in the garden, but I'm not listening. I dive back into the house and return with a baseball bat. It's ridiculously big, cartoon style in its proportions, but I can lift it easily.

I run towards Sam, with the bat bouncing on my shoulder and he doesn't try to run away. He is still standing with his hands outstretched, a childlike look of bewilderment on his pale face. He's still talking to me, still trying to calm me down. But I simply raise the bat and belt him as hard as I can across his head. At this point, the family drop their glasses in unison and begin to flit around what is left of the garden, because they can't actually pass me while I'm wielding my gigantic baseball bat – I might hit one of them accidentally. So they dash about in mixed groups of young and old, clutching onto each other with white-knuckled little hands, and they watch me batter my husband to the ground.

One or two of them shout out to me to stop hitting him, but I don't hear them. I'm far too intent on smashing Sam's fat face into the grass and I carry on belting him time and time again.

I realise how terrifically strong I must be to be able to floor a man who is six feet four inches tall and weighs 23 stones. After all, I am a mere scrap of humanity at five feet, and my entire weight equals that of his left leg. He is kneeling pathetically in front of me now with his family screeching with terror at the sight before them. They are all crying, mascara-streaked faces everywhere. Meanwhile, Sam is sobbing into the earth and still attempting to communicate, but every time he lifts his stupid balding head to speak, I give it another satisfying whack with my baseball bat . . .

When all is quiet out in the garden, and the family have escaped into the street, scurrying away in several directions, Sam has managed to prop himself against the lawnmower. He is covered in champagne, bits of glass and dog piss. I suddenly appear and survey the scene before me. I kneel down in front of him, and I look into his blood-streaked face. He averts his eyes to begin with, but eventually returns my gaze. And then, I say the one sentence that justifies the whole incident. 'Well darlin, none of this would have happened if you hadn't left that lawnmower out, now would it?' And he nods quietly in agreement. And then I add, 'But you know I didn't mean to hurt you sweetheart. You know that I love you, don't you?'

The tape rewound itself again, and despite my trying to think of other things, it began to play that morning's scenes complete with background sound and accompanying heartbreak.

CHAPTER TWO

Of course, it wasn't always like that. I can remember catching my breath at the very sound of his voice over the phone, and how I actually ached for him when we weren't together. Yes, the day I fell for Sam Brown was the day I actually thought I'd finally hit the jackpot as far as finding my ideal man was concerned. When I was 26 I worked in the Edinburgh branch of an office supplies firm. As jobs go, it was somewhat boring, the product being particularly uninteresting to me. Pens, paper and sellotape never quite inspired me to build a career around them, but there were plenty who enjoyed selling anything, with the main object being to reach their monthly targets. My job title was Inside Salesperson and Typist. It was a small office in Leith, just two streets away from my home so the convenience made up for its tendency to bore.

I was a hard-working single mother, with two small boys to bring up. In lots of ways, however, I considered myself lucky. I had my job, which seemed secure, and I was pleased with our small tenement flat which I had waited over two years for on the housing list. My mother Kathy shared the flat with us, and looked after David who was four years old and Ryan who was three, while I went out to work for us all. Mum, a fit and energetic sixty-year-old, was an excellent housekeeper and cook, she is also my best friend and confidante. She has a natural skill in caring for her grandsons whom she loves dearly. They in turn dote on their fun-loving Nana and both boys were happy and secure in their little world,

Money was always a problem as my wages were not good, despite my having specific qualifications for the job and its trade. But, Mum had brought my brother Malcolm and me up as a single parent during the 1960s and things were even worse for one-parent families then. As a result, my memories of never having anything extra, and the constant monotony of being skint were always with me. I had decided almost from the start of my first job after leaving high school that I would budget my money carefully so that, although it was spread thinly throughout the month, I would also be saving up for something big as well. Mum had her pension and, although she could keep it to herself, she often contributed towards the housekeeping. I could go out whenever I liked, either with or without the children, and Mum had her friends and family that she could go out with on occasion. We even had a luxury, in the shape of a Mini Metro car called Bluey, which was its metallic colour.

My ex-husband Keith also lived in Edinburgh and worked in Leith. We had met when I was 16 and he was 23, and he was my first boyfriend, my first real love. As a teenager I had no social life whatsoever. In 1980 I worked as an office junior in a firm situated in the city centre but I lived on the seventh floor of a block of flats on the outskirts of Edinburgh. The girls that I chatted to during the day in the office all seemed to live in the city and while they were preparing for yet another wild weekend I would be preparing for my exhausting double bus journey out of the Capital towards home. I never knew any of them closely enough to stay the night with them, should they invite me out somewhere, and the thought of having to leave some heaving club before ten o'clock to catch the last bus put me off the idea anyway.

So, content with spending my early teenage years indoors with Mum for company, there were few chances to meet any boys. I started a diary, initially to be written in only on a Sunday, the most boring day of my week by far. It was the friend I didn't have really, and I moaned incessantly, secure in the knowledge that my complaining scribbles would never be commented upon. I could even write down the unspeakable thoughts that invaded my adolescent mind, usually about other people. Keith lived only two doors away from us at the time, and was unemployed when we met. He would take an unskilled manual job on one month and leave it, without a second thought, the next if something about it upset him. He would regard it a personal snub if his foreman offered him more hours of work, and he would simply leave the area without further discussion. I remember being horrified when he told me he had walked out of his job only six weeks after he had started there, and he was adamant that he was quite justified in resigning after some trivial incident.

While the unemployment figures remained alarmingly high, each new career move for Keith meant longer periods of being out of work and, of course, shorter periods when he would actually stay in a job. He was heavy-set in build, and was considered a good-looking young man. He had light brown hair and striking blue eyes and unusually, considering the fashion at the time, he sported a glorious red beard. He was fairly uneducated and somewhat immature but made good company for me and we quickly fell in love. With a boyfriend at last, I was excited and had rosy thoughts of our future together. Keith was nothing like any of the male members of my family and he seemed caring and kind. Nobody, however, thought that we were suited to each other, but I considered myself strong enough to solve any problem that could arise. I could always work for the two of us, I could always be sociable and I would be the mature and sensible one who would put everything into our marriage to help make it a success.

We were married in October 1982, when I was 18 years old and Dexy's Midnight Runners were belting out 'Come on Eileen' on every radio. On the morning of our wedding day I stood looking into the mirror in my bedroom before putting on my beautiful dress. I asked myself if I really knew what I was doing – considering everything honestly. I answered, yes, even although I knew that I no longer actually loved Keith. I reckoned that I could live with him and raise a family. He was, I concluded, better than nothing, and without him I would probably have nothing again, and a brief snatch of my lonely, boring teenage years entered my mind.

We bought a flat in Leith with a mortgage from the Council. Two years later our son David was born, 17 days late, but very much welcomed. Keith became involved with the baby and could change the dirtiest nappy and made up bottles without complaint. We would take turns in getting up at night, since our family routine was hardly a traditional one. Other young mothers with children of a similar age would prattle on about how they felt they must deal with the baby during the wee small hours, while Daddy lay snoring in peace, since he was the one who got up at seven o'clock five days a week to go out to work till six at night. I'd praise Keith's 'New Man' attitude to family life instead of just telling the truth about his aversion to working at any point after lunchtime, any day of the week!

Now that I was at home looking after David we were completely dependent on Keith's meagre earnings. Some weeks, when he worked as a window cleaner with a small firm in the city, he would come home with an underwhelming pay packet of just £30. Our weekly shopping bill for the three of us came to that amount alone. Careful budgeting and strict spending limits kept us from debt and we managed to scrape along. In an effort to improve our situation, I suggested to Keith that we try to sell the flat and put the profit together with a small redundancy payment I'd received from my last office job into a small business. However, when we'd sold the flat, and were living with Mum in her high-rise flat in Wester Hailes, we calculated that we really didn't have enough money to buy even a lease on a newsagent's business.

I became pregnant, not because I felt that the future would be secure, or even that Keith and I were close to resolving any of the problems that we now had, but because I wanted another baby. It was as simple as that. Keith was neither surprised nor pleased at the prospect of another baby. By that point, though, I really didn't care about his lack of opinion on the subject, since it would hardly affect him anyway. It wasn't as if he hitched up his jeans, and complained about the amount of overtime he'd have to put in to keep us in the manner to which we had become accustomed. He continued to work from 8 a.m. until about 1 p.m. on dry days, but lying full length on the settee in front of a blaring television if it rained.

In July 1986, I was nearly five months pregnant and working full time in the shop Mum and I had opened which sold second-hand bridalwear. I'd spend all day selling beautiful 'only worn once' wedding dresses, veils and bridesmaid's outfits to girls – similar in age – who were preparing for their once-in-a-lifetime weddings. Meanwhile, I was seriously considering ending my own marriage.

We eventually separated the following month, with Keith moving out of Mum's house almost immediately, and staying at his Mum's. After the initial shock of my blunt suggestion one morning, before I travelled into Leith to open the shop, he had more or less agreed that he had thought about the idea himself towards the end. He didn't like staying at Mum's house, wasn't particularly keen on having another baby anyway, and had concluded that he wasn't prepared to change his working habits for me or the children. I assured him that he would not be kept from seeing David, and the baby if he felt the need, and asked only that he pay some money weekly towards their upkeep, which I knew would be much less than he was having to hand over in housekeeping.

Keith very quickly acquired a girlfriend, and as I had suspected, his visits to see David became less frequent. Ryan arrived one December afternoon, with remarkable ease and little effort on my part. I was always fit and healthy during my pregnancies, and gave birth to Ryan so quickly and without complications, that I was proudly taking him home to Wester Hailes the very next day.

By the following May, Keith was happily entrenched at his girlfriend Joyce's home, and his weekly payments of £20 had dried up completely. One weekend, he didn't arrive to take David out, and he made no attempt to see any of his children ever again. I bravely accepted the situation and decided that the boys could well do without a father who could hardly spell the word 'responsibility' let alone aspire to it. Anyway, I knew I could cope – and Mum supported me with the business and the children. Keith was very awkward about agreeing to a divorce because he did not want to pay maintenance for children in whom he had no further interest. Despite his lawyer's attempts to make him aware of his duty towards his children, he plodded along relentlessly for four years before his lawyers eventually refused to represent him and he lost his case.

When I had been offered the tenancy of our two-bedroomed flat in Leith Mum and I were over the moon about the prospect of living in the city once more. The high flats in Wester Hailes were gradually being abandoned by tenants sick of living in its run-down council estate. The community was disintegrating, and it seemed that the council delayed carrying out repairs to anything and everything – as if they were making up their minds about what they could do with the entire area.

Our street in Leith still had some tenants who had actually been born and brought up there. Now they congregated in little groups at the front gates of the church, taking head counts in case one of them had died since the last time they'd met. Wizened old ladies walked sedately past our stair, kicking Coke cans out of their way and snarling at the local dogs which watched their progress. However, chatting to one of two sisters who lived in our stair, I was transported back 60 years to a time when the same wizened creature skipped cheerily past the same stair, with plaits in her long hair and mud streaks down her legs, jam around her mouth from that morning's breakfast and her future still invitingly unknown. Our boys were the only children in the entire stair and the old residents, their husbands long dead, made a point of talking to them whenever they met.

Ryan, now two years old, was the most sociable child and would insist on a cuddle from these old women who lived around us – which of course endeared him to them instantly. David, at three, was attending a speech therapist, because everyone, including ourselves, had difficulty in understanding a single word he said. Since he was hopefully going to be attending nursery school, the authorities and I felt we should get as much help as possible in improving his speech. Both boys were biddable in character and pleasant in manner, and very well behaved. Neighbours' compliments on such beautiful boys made me proud and assured that I must at least be doing something right in life. So there I was, in a great flat, with my lovely family, my ever-helpful mother, and a full-time job and a car for weekend trips away with the boys. I had a lot to be grateful for.

CHAPTER THREE

In February 1990 my days were brightened by the now frequent exchange of phone calls from Sam, my opposite number who worked for a rival firm, also in Edinburgh. As with most trades, we knew who our rivals were, and who worked in the offices. Sometimes we would find ourselves attending the same college courses and at the worst, if your position became redundant – you could find yourself approaching these rival companies for employment. So, we remained polite and respectful towards them, despite the fact that we each tried to poach the other's business.

Tuesday, 13 February 1990
Valentine's Day tomorrow, and it'll be a bare doormat again – except for the odd bill I bet. I was asked out for a blind date, but turned it down on the spur – and kind of regretted it soon after. It's almost automatic now to avoid male contact, when I really would like to do some dating again. Must be premonition or something . . .

Sam had a voice like chocolate, deep and smooth and slightly cultured. I had only been in the job for seven months, having closed the shop the year before. Going back into the office supplies business had felt much like going home for me and familiar aspects of the job gave me the confidence to work full time. Sam had been with his firm since he'd left school at 16. This impressed me. I felt it showed loyalty and dedication. He asked if I was married and I jokingly remarked 'Why, are you asking?' and without hesitation, he said 'Yes'. We hurriedly set a date – 7 July, and giggled about how we would recognise each other. He suggested we meet for a drink before the big day, but I refused again. I'd never been out on a 'blind date' and really didn't want to be seen out with 'one of the enemy', however innocent it actually was.

Sunday, 4 March 1990
Went out with my blind date yesterday! His name is Sam and he is my opposite man at one of our main competitors. He's 29, single, 'enormous' in height and girth, seems homely, normal, great sense of humour – (well, he makes me laugh anyway) and like me, doesn't have much of a social life. We had a lovely lunch, and a wander in the city, but when I suggested it was time for me getting home to the boys, he affectionately kissed my forehead and blurted out something like 'we must do this again sometime'. Never asked for my home number, another date or even another conversation come Monday. I presume I bored him and he was only too grateful to be getting on his train (he lives in Stirling). Meanwhile, I sauntered down Leith Street sighing wistfully, and wondered just how strong was my BO anyway . . .

He was back on the phone to me by Monday afternoon though, apparently eager to arrange another date for that evening, and we met in a pub not far from his office in the city. His size was overwhelming. He was not only tall at six feet four inches, but his self-description of 'heavily built' could be translated into 'overweight'. His padded winter jacket made his girth seem even wider and I felt small and childlike beside him as we walked together.

We chatted effortlessly, Sam buying all the drinks while I felt myself relax into the evening. He still lived at home with his Mum and two brothers. Sam was the oldest. His father had died tragically at the age of 47 and his mother had bravely soldiered on, looking after 'her boys' as if it was her sole duty in life. (I found out later that it was.) Sam had had previous girlfriends, and had almost married one. Things had fallen apart quite suddenly not long after his father's death. He asked about my marriage, and about the boys. I showed him the few photographs I carried about in my purse and he studied them with interest, but without comment. He tutted with disgust at Keith's complete lack of interest in the children, remarking on the loss the boys might feel not now, but later perhaps. I presumed he was referring to the loss of his own father. The night sped by, and I wished time would crawl once more, so that I could enjoy more of this man's company.

Tuesday, 20 March 1990

We go out about three times a week – early nights, because he has about two hours travelling to do before he gets home. After a night out with him I'm on a high – and I think about him all the time. He's intelligent, mature, sensible, funny, romantic and understanding. He is handsome (but fat) and I love his accent, his deep voice (he does a cracking Sean Connery impression). He met the boys, and they just love him. Shy to begin with, but he's a real natural with them. I warned him that I'm a bit of a traditionalist when it comes to behaviour, but he says he is the eldest of four boys, and he's used to children around. He is relaxed and spontaneous with their play. Things are getting very serious. I hate it when he has to leave for Stirling, and when it's time to drive up into Edinburgh to meet him after work, my stomach turns with excitement. I recognise this from Keith.

I can't sleep, can't eat, am a bit on edge, but think that's just the excitement. Wouldn't it be great to be in love for the rest of your days? Last night he told me that he was falling in love with me – God I felt great! Mum seems pleased that I've found someone to go out with. She likes the way he sends me a single rose, or perhaps a card with a poem inside – but I don't know if she knows the depth of things yet.

So, we'll see where this all takes us. It may end within the month, year or whatever. As long as I enjoy it – it's a bonus.

One night I asked Sam about the girlfriend he was engaged to be married to. He shook his head slowly, and took a deep breath before recounting the story. Linda was only 16 when they had met, Sam being 26 at the time. He was working in her home city of Newcastle and when they had decided to live together, Sam had elected to settle down back in Scotland and had applied to return to his branch in Edinburgh. He and Linda bought a cottage in Fife and secured a loan to buy a car for them both to cope with travelling in and out of Edinburgh each day. She gained employment in the city and all was going well towards a summer wedding in the August of 1989 when she suddenly packed her bags and left for Newcastle one day.

Sam had been both shocked and surprised by this and had immediately set about trying to find her. According to him, there had been no arguments or even a petty row, and she had never expressed any fears about their impending marriage not working. Linda did return to their cottage, and had settled in again until Sam's father died so suddenly at the family home just two months before the wedding. The family were devastated. Sam and his brothers Derek, Lawrence and Andrew had loved and admired their Dad who had worked reliably for years in various unskilled, manual jobs around Central Scotland to keep his large family and wife from the clutches of poverty.

Sam's manner became quiet and thoughtful as he told me that he had decided one evening to go to his local for a drink and Linda had preferred to stay at the cottage to tidy up. On his return, the lights were on but there was no sign of her. Her clothes were gone from the wardrobes and drawers: she had run away again. He said that it had broken his heart, and this time she was not returning. She abandoned everything and left Sam with cancelling the arrangements for the wedding. The car had to be sold and, because he could no longer afford the mortgage on the cottage himself, he had simply handed it back to the building society. He said he had been left with considerable debt, which he was paying off gradually, but since all this had happened only seven months or so before we had met, he said he was only just beginning to recover from it all. He felt hurt and aggrieved at her immature actions.

I sympathised with him, and offered my theory as to why she couldn't go through with the wedding. He offered no explanation other than that she was, in his opinion, too young to cope with the monotony of living and working towards a permanent future. I really felt sorry for him – and I accepted the entire story as he told it, which seemed plausible, and sad.

Saturday, 31 March 1990
Caught some damned cold – probably from kissing Sam since he had a slight cold too. We only saw each other twice last week, which was agony. Wish he stayed in Edinburgh. I'm

absolutely potty about this guy, can't believe he's here. Already I'm feeling broody and wish we could set up house together with the boys.

I'd feel so safe with him. He seems to be so rock steady, I just love him to bits. I am doubtful though, I mean, I could probably look back through my diaries and see that I've written the same slush about Keith. For instance, sometimes, he'll say exactly the same phrase that Keith said. I know that Keith and I did love each other at some point, but essentially I made a really bad choice. Now, I know that I haven't even spent an entire month with Sam, but I think I want to spend the rest of my life with him. We've arranged to take our summer holidays together. I think the boys will love it. We are going to the Lake District, for one week, and Mum is already looking forward to the peace and quiet. It'll be a good tester for us – see how we get on being together for an entire week. I must enjoy the present, and forget the bad old past. I wish I could see into the future though.

Roll on July . . .

I saved avidly throughout the spring time, but still enjoyed romantic evenings in the city during the week, and adventure-filled weekends with the children. They chattered endlessly about Sam, and I knew they were growing fond of him. When I brought him home to meet Mum, they seemed to get on almost immediately. He was his usual charming and humorous self, and Mum remarked on his adoring attitude towards me. She also thought he was good with the boys, who were by this time practically crawling over him as soon as he appeared. David would sit beside Sam, gazing up at him adoringly. He would save particular paintings or drawings for Sam to marvel at, and sat smiling bashfully when he praised his efforts. Similar touching scenes made me realise that perhaps the lad remembered his father more than I had given him credit for. David went to nursery, where he would entertain his teachers with tall stories about his latest adventure with 'Dad Sam'. His Dad Sam was an airforce pilot, who would sometimes allow David to sit on his lap while they jetted off to the supermarket together. Of course, Dad Sam would then buy him lots of everything, and more if he wanted, and they would journey home, flying over the Forth

Bridges, just for the ride. The teachers raved about his imagination, and encouraged me to support his efforts through his drawing and painting.

Ryan was also fond of Sam, but he lacked the thirst for attention that his brother had. More physical in his play, and eager to be the strongest and fastest at everything, he found it difficult to sit and sketch for an hour. He loved to be jokingly manhandled by Sam, and would happily sit high on his shoulders enjoying the height and the feeling of power that went with it. He would sit comfortably on Sam's knee while they watched television together but almost unconsciously he would slip off Sam's legs and wander across the room, to nestle beside me on my chair. He showed a loyalty towards his mother and his Nana that seemed to irk Sam somehow. It was as if the boy should submit totally to his charm and appeal, just as his mother and brother had already done.

We would plan trips and picnics at the weekends, using Bluey for transport. Sam had eventually forced himself to get into the car after initially refusing any offers of a lift from me. Almost immediately, it was obvious that he didn't consider me a good driver and he made a very bad passenger. He would stop talking at junctions so that he could 'ghost drive' me through them. Sometimes he would cover his eyes if he thought I was driving too fast, too slow or too close to something. His nerves made me doubt my driving ability, never before commented on by anybody. I insisted that I had been driving for seven accident-free years, and that I was confident and able, but he would not be convinced. Although he never actually came out and said that he thought me incompetent behind the wheel, I eventually let him drive Bluey everywhere.

By the end of April, Sam had decided to begin looking for a suitable flat to rent in Edinburgh. This would save time in commuting to and from work every day and would make a difference financially too. Our nights out wouldn't have to be cut short because of the one-and-a-half-hour trip back to Stirling on the last train and bus. According to Sam, his mother Marjery had been pleased to hear of her son's move from the family home. When I eventually met her, one incredibly wet Sunday, I thought she was friendly and welcoming towards myself and the boys. We met in the house that Sam had actually been born in, and she had lived in the same street since she had been a girl. She was overweight and unhealthy with it and looked much older than the 50 years that she claimed to be. She insisted that her size was due to a family physical characteristic, that they were all 'heavy built', and she criticised someone who had mentioned only the other week, that she could be overeating and not getting enough exercise. She walked with the aid of a stick, since her back gave her constant pain. She was able to climb the stairs within her house only three times a day, since she huffed and puffed like an asthmatic, though she never smoked. Her day consisted of rising at 6 a.m. to make her sons' breakfasts, then doing their laundry and the general housework downstairs. Her hobby was knitting, and the monthly shopping was done by one of the boys on the appropriate weekend. If they were going out at night, Marjery would receive orders as to which items of clothes were to be washed and ironed, and if one of them stumbled in drunk, Marjery would be there, waiting up for them in the living-room. She missed her husband Ian immensely, since there was never much conversation from Lawrence or Derek. She would chatter on endlessly whenever we went to visit, sometimes about what a neighbour had said, or about an item of news she had seen on television. She could fill a whole hour on the difference between one knitting pattern and another – and she would press us to stay a little longer, if we made signs that we would like to go. She admitted that she would miss Sam's company (I presume he could listen to her with a bit more patience than his brothers) but was glad to see him settling nearer his work and us. 'Of course, he would have been well settled by now, if that stupid lassie had stayed with him,' she commented thoughtfully.

'Why do you think she left then?' This was a chance to find out about a subject that Sam now kept closed.

'Too young. I mean, when I was a girl there was nae chance of any career. You just left school, took a job in a shop and went out every weekend till you met a laddie that wanted to settle wi' ye. Linda was only 18 when they bought that cottage together, I mean, she wasnae ready to settle down wi' him, gettin' married and huvin' bairns.'

'Some way to end a relationship though, Just walking out like that.' I felt I was sounding nosey, but I really wanted to know her opinion about Linda. Sam came back into the room, and had obviously caught the end of my question to his mum.

'She was bloody lucky I never kicked her out, stupid bitch that she was.'

'Och well . . .' Marjery began, as she attempted to shuffle herself from the confines of her chair, 'that's all behind you now, and I think you've met your match in Susan,' and she winked at me while she awaited his reaction. There was none.

Sunday, 13 May 1990

Skint as usual. Just as well Sam pays for our nights out, otherwise we would do nothing all month. He's found a flat to rent, and moves into it in less than a fortnight. I cannot wait. The boys are pleased because they'll see more of him at the weekends. He wants to settle down. He says that he wants to leave his office at night, and come home to the boys and me. It's what I want too. We've been discussing house hunting for ourselves, and he says that if we can just wait until his cottage is sold then we can start thinking about it seriously. I really think this guy is the one for me (and the kids). I think he is ready to settle down, and wants to work for us, and protect us as his family. I sometimes just cannot believe that I've found him, and that the kids love him so much too is such a bonus! I'm sure that with his help and support they will progress and mature. And, if we have a family of our own, I think he'd make a great dad . . .

Meanwhile, my office had been one of the branches successful in achieving a sales target which would earn us a good bonus payout. I excitedly told Sam about it, and decided to save almost all of it (£1,200) to put down as a deposit on our first home together.

Mum was thrilled at the thought of me moving into a bought house with Sam and the boys as a family. She had always hoped that I would find the right man to partner me in helping to bring up her grandsons. We discussed the mechanics of transferring the house tenancy over to her name, and I assured her that we would try to buy a place close to her street, so that the kids could still see their Nana daily.

Not long after Sam had moved all his possessions from Stirling and put his flat into some kind of order, we had our first tiff. It was getting close to the end of his salary month, and he was getting short of cash. I had suggested a night out somewhere, and he refused almost immediately. He seemed a bit down and despondent. Later that evening, I decided that since he was always paying for everything, including the deposit for our holiday in July, I would lend him some money to tide him over. I duly trotted off towards the cash machine, and smartly pushed a plump envelope through his letterbox. I tip-toed away from his door, imagining him being surprised and happy about the money he'd find inside the package. After only five minutes back inside my own house, there was an officious knock at the front door.

'There's your bloody money, you can keep it. I'm hardly a charity case,' he announced. 'If you want to talk about this further, you know where I am.'

He stomped off petulantly, while I remained static, still holding the door open, almost as wide as my mouth.

Sunday, 27 May 1990
There will be bloody cobwebs on him before I go around there to apologise! I don't understand this stupid show of pride. Is he trying to say that I insulted him by giving back some of the money I owe him (we were to go halves on the holiday deposit anyway), and that he'd rather be skint and miserable. Well, good luck to him! I can be depressed about that myself, without having him crashing about with a torn face. I'm hurting a bit though. I hope he phones me about it, because I don't see that I deserve that kind of treatment . . .

Monday afternoon saw a large bunch of flowers delivered to the flat, with an accompanying message saying 'sorry'. He didn't go into detail about the money incident, and I presumed that it was just a bout of stress that had clouded his normally charming character.

Our planned week's holiday was a roaring success. The boys had a great time and the weather was kind to us. Sam remained attentive and interested in David and Ryan's achievements, and would spend time including them in his own hobbies. Sam was good with his hands, and enjoyed building model aeroplanes. He bought inexpensive toy ones for each boy, and spent most of one day trying to show them how to launch them properly.

He showed a patience and understanding of them both which

put me at ease, whereas before I found myself watchful over his attitude towards the boys. Even Mum had commented that his intention towards the boys couldn't still be false, after all this time. He admitted that he had grown to love my children, and I believed that he did.

By the beginning of August, Sam's sudden bouts of huffiness were becoming more frequent, and I found them tiresome and petty.

3 August 1990
Still falling in and out with each other, but I still look at him and think how much I love him. We quarrel at least once a fortnight. What is amazing, is that these arguments are over such trivial things. I get wound up and upset about them, and he apologises at the drop of a hat and expects me to forget about it! Take his jacket for instance. He's worn this thick padded winter coat every day since I've met him. It's summer, and folk are walking about in shorts and T shirts, but not Sam. Regardless of the temperature, he has his heavy jacket on. He insists he is not bothered about his weight (he is maybe three stone overweight) but cannot bear to be without at least two layers of clothing to cover his bulk! The sweat is dribbling off him! We were just about to pop down to a superstore one afternoon, and I casually mentioned that he could do without his jacket for a change. God . . . you'd think I'd asked him to eat it! Then, he goes into a kind of huff, and can't bring himself to speak for an hour or two. Then, all of a sudden, he's fine . . .

Sometimes Sam would deny himself any contact with me for an entire day, if we were both at work and then he'd phone me at home that evening either to apologise or to discuss our next night out together. If I challenged him to discuss his last bout of huffiness, he would sometimes deny that anything other than a normal evening had occurred.

One morning I had travelled into my office as usual, only to be faced with stricken-featured colleagues milling about outside. The news was bad, the office had been closed, and we were to be merged with a larger, more cost-efficient firm. Jobs had been cut, mine included. After the initial shock, I set about selling Bluey, which was sad, and I realised I would have to begin dipping into my savings towards the deposit for a house. We made one last trip up to Stirling to visit Marjery before the car was sold. While Sam was sitting slouched in his chair, reading a newspaper, Marjery remembered something that she had found somewhere in the house, and mentioned it to Sam.

'Oh aye,' he answered with enthusiasm, and he sat himself up straight in his chair, while Marjery disappeared from the room. She returned smiling, and holding a heavy sheepskin jacket.

'Try it on,' they both chorused, and Marjery held it out for me. I thought it was very nice, perhaps not my first choice in jackets, but it looked new. I was actually in the process of trying to save up for a winter coat for the coming season.

'I bought it for that cow. Christ, anything that caught her eye, she bloody wanted it. She never wore it . . . well, maybe once,' Sam said. They both approved and admired the coat on me, but I quietly took it off, claiming that I didn't like the fit. Inside I was simmering gently with anger. The coat had been Linda's. She hadn't worn it enough to justify the amount of money Sam had spent on her, so it seemed it would make him feel better if I got some wear out of it. Didn't I deserve a new jacket? I also noted the scathing attitude that both Sam and his mother referred to Linda. They couldn't even say her name.

We snapped at each other sarcastically all the way home in the car. The boys slept innocently in the back seat, as I tried to point out Sam's insensitive and tactless track of thought behind his offer of the coat. He couldn't see my point though, and the car accelerated steadily, along with his boiling anger. I dropped the argument completely, and we continued the journey home in silence. When he parked Bluey, he promptly got out of the car, and walked towards his street. I let him.

Mum agreed with me about my reasons for not accepting the jacket. Later, I remarked on Sam's apparent disrespect for his mother. On that day, it had been particularly noticeable. He would sit himself down, and proceed to leaf through her Sunday papers, while Marjery chatted to me and the children. Occasionally, she would talk directly to him, especially if the subject involved someone that he knew. If she interrupted his concentration while reading something, he would quite blatantly tell her to 'give it a rest'. If she had an opinion about something that was clearly important to her, and she tried to explain it to him, he would sometimes cut her dead by ordering her out of the room to make us coffee or something.

'And what does Marjery say, when he does that?' Mum asked with interest.

'Not a word. It's as if she doesn't notice.'

'She's probably let them treat her like that for the past 30 years; better watch he doesn't start treating you in the same manner.'

'No chance,' I shot back confidently, 'I'm bloody sure I would notice if one of my children tried to speak to me like that, and I certainly wouldn't let Sam try it on me. Not even once.'

I reflected on his bitter attitude towards Linda, coupled with the obvious disrespect he showed towards his own mother. For such an apparently sensitive and understanding man, the cracks in his veneer were displaying a certain dislike of women in general. I assumed, though, that I was not one of them.

CHAPTER FOUR

Throughout the rest of that year I constantly asked myself if I could really live with a man like Sam. We were hoping to be house hunting for our own flat in the new year, and as that step towards some kind of commitment to each other drew closer, I found myself examining him as a person, and eventual husband.

I loved him, I knew that much. I realised that he had some kind of problem when he would take offence at something rather trivial. He always found a way to apologise though, which I counted on as important at the time. He was very good with the boys, He was a hard worker. He wanted to settle down and was anxious to find a home to buy for us, even although I was now unemployed. Compared with Keith, Sam still came out way ahead. We really did get on well, when he wasn't in a huff with me. We could still laugh and talk together. We still craved each other's company. We seemed to agree about different aspects of David and Ryan's upbringing, and also in our attitude towards money and saving. Although I found Sam's petty huffs annoying and tiresome, I was aware that having to put up with them (presuming they didn't actually get worse) on a day-to-day basis, for the rest of our lives, would be some challenge.

Sometimes, if something had annoyed him sufficiently to warrant a 'stomping-off episode' I would decide to wait the usual amount of time it took him to come to apologise, and I would smartly throw it back in his face. I'd tell him how sick I was of his petty little tantrums, and that it was about time he'd outgrown them. This seemed to send him into a kind of panic, and he would phone frantically, asking to speak to me, pleading to be forgiven. He would agree that the particular reason for his

31

temper tantrum was rather paltry, and he would explain that he didn't really know why such small matters should affect him in such a way.

Mum was also baffled by his behaviour, but suggested that maybe it was his way of testing the relationship. 'He'll probably settle down and give up arguing over insignificant details once you are living together,' she offered.

The only real friends of Sam's that I ever met were Mhari and Graham. They had both gone to school with Sam in his home town, and had married and gone to live just outside Edinburgh. They thought the world of their childhood friend. Mhari and I seemed to get on well, and I enjoyed her sense of humour. She told me how awful it had been for Sam when Linda had left, and she waited until Sam and Graham were out of range before she would discuss Sam's past with me.

'Of course, she was just a gold-digger,' she announced, as she preened herself in front of her mirror. 'She was far too young, and stupid with it, you know, a smile on a stick really. I think once Sam stopped taking her everywhere and paying for everything, and started to save up for the house and the wedding, she decided she'd get out of it before things became legal.' She glanced at her own wedding rings, and buffed them up with the rib of her lambswool jersey.

'Sam can fly off into a temper at the drop of a hat mind. I suppose Linda was a bit too immature to cope with it.' I watched Mhari's expression closely once I'd finished my sentence. She looked directly at me.

'Well, I've known Sam for over 20 years, and I don't think I've ever seen him even slightly annoyed. He's a great guy, Susan, an absolute gem. He just needs someone who loves him, and cares for him, who is sensible and genuine. Couldn't exactly call Linda genuine, I don't think she cared about him at all, or she wouldn't have swanned off like that.' She continued to refer to Sam in positive terms only. She and Marjery were really the only people I could glean any inside information about Sam from.

His brothers, Derek and Lawrence, who still lived with their mother, were nearly always still in their beds whenever we visited on a Sunday. Andrew lived in his own flat nearby and was rarely at his mother's house anyway. On the odd occasion that the brothers were up and about they showed their ignorance by not even acknowledging our presence in the house. It seemed too much to ask for any kind of greeting, and their obvious disinterest in myself and the children was blatant. I tried to initiate conversation the first few times we met, by asking after girlfriends and showing interest in their respective jobs. Eventually, though, I grew just as rude, and learned to ignore them as well. I shared my disbelief at their behaviour with Sam who agreed at first, sometimes showing embarrassment at their failure to hold an intelligible conversation.

So, it was with a reasonably clear mind, and a positive attitude towards our future, that we began applying for a mortgage during January 1991.

A vacancy arose within the outside sales force at Sam's firm. He was duly promoted, receiving an increase in salary and a much treasured company car. There were no problems with his earnings not being sufficient enough for the mortgage amount we needed.

I smiled smugly at the stark contrasts between Keith and Sam and their abilities to earn a decent wage. It was another reason to go ahead and set up home with him. The more people that knew about our plans, the more encouraged I felt about our relationship.

We began house hunting, and quickly settled on a small two-bedroomed flat situated in a new housing estate close to our present home.

Monday, 28 January 1991

The flat is ours! We put in our offer, and it's all run so smoothly, it's unreal. We went into the office to sign for the mortgage applications etc and we should get the keys to our first home at the beginning of March. Sam and I are over the moon, and the boys are so excited. They'll still be able to attend the same school and nursery, so it won't be such an upheaval for them. We are making plans and looking forward to it so much, I just cannot wait for the next six weeks to pass! everyone is so pleased for us. I'm so glad that I saved up the money I got before I lost my job, since that's what really helped us to buy the flat. Of course, Sam's wages will have to pay for the mortgage, until I get some kind of part-time job. I think he realises that things will be tough to begin with, and really, that's the price he'll have to pay to have us all living together. Both our names are on the mortgage papers though (apparently his was the only one, the last time he bought the cottage with Linda) so at least I know he can't try to throw me out, if things go bad . . .

While waiting to move into the flat, Sam again exploded over another incident, and this time I really stood back to examine our future together.

It was a clear, crisp Saturday morning, and Sam and I thought we would take David and Ryan out for a drive to a park near a DIY store Sam wanted to look at. Despite my being insured to drive it, Sam rarely allowed me to take charge of the wheel while he was in the car. He preferred to drive it himself. But on this day, he casually nodded when I asked if I could drive, and he suggested we take a quick look around our estate to catch a glimpse of the flat we would soon be moving into. The houses were situated at the end of a wide cobbled road and as we neared our flat Sam pointed it out for the boys to see and they sat straining their eyes, looking at all the windows in our block, while I slowly drove past. I decided to turn the car and, since there was no traffic anywhere, I swung the vehicle around so that it would face the other direction. On doing so, however, one wheel went up onto the pavement, and gently bumped us down again into the gutter. As soon as it happened, Sam practically 'blew up' beside me in the passenger seat.

'You stupid bitch,' he roared, 'what a bloody way to drive, Christ, it could have been a wall, a person or anything!' The boys were stunned into silence, their eyes wide with fear.

'It was just the kerb, it was an accident, Sam. For God's sake,' I shouted back.

'You're a fucking idiot!' he screamed at me, before getting out of the car altogether. I was shaking with both fear and absolute rage at his display, and I glanced back at both children who were beginning to cry.

'It's okay,' I tried to assure them, with a breaking voice. 'Daddy Sam is just pretending to be a baby this morning. Mummy didn't really do anything wrong,' but I started up the car (which had actually stalled, due to his tantrum taking me by surprise) and held the wheel so tight with anger that my knuckles were white. I drove past Sam as he walked towards his flat, and promised the boys that they would still be going to the park, only without Daddy Sam.

Saturday, 9 February 1991

. . . so he stomped off (yet again) and ruined what could have been a lovely day out with the kids. Poor David was crying, they were both shocked and dismayed to see their Mum and Dad Sam fighting like that. And over what? I mean, am I really so inept? I'm certain he's driven up onto a kerb before, and I don't hit the bloody roof like he does! Stupid man. I dropped off the car in front of his house (after I'd been to the park with the children) and went in to tell him what a prat he'd been. He just stood there, with a 'well are you finished now' kind of look while I shouted at him. God, this is giving me cold feet about moving in with him. Imagine if he does this every day. Imagine the boys being frightened to move, or say something in case Daddy does his bloody nut over something. God I'm worried now. Mum is thinking about exchanging our house for a one-bedroomed one. My bridges are being burnt behind me now – what if I'm making a mistake in living with Sam? Maybe now is the time I should back out . . . . pretty much like Linda did, eh?

At home I felt tearful and anxious. I warned Mum about putting her plans on hold for the time being, since I had no idea what the situation between Sam and I was. In three weeks' time we would be jointly signing papers that would give us ownership of our own home. Joint mortgage, joint bills and, hopefully, joint commitment to each other.

'The amazing thing about us, Mum, is that we get on so well together, we actually enjoy each other's company. And, he's kind, considerate, affectionate, understanding, can take a joke, can make me laugh – and then, all of a sudden, he loses his temper over the tiniest detail that you or I would hardly notice! I can appreciate that he may be under a bit of stress just now, with his new job and buying the flat, but he doesn't think that after we settle in there will be nothing left to get stressed about, surely?'

'Well, men can be like little boys sometimes. They're upset about something, but it's too petty to discuss it with you, so they create some tension about the house until you actually ask them "what's wrong?" Sam certainly didn't have any right to act the way he did in the car, the boys adore him, and he was wrong to frighten them like that. Sounds as if he's a bit immature, if you ask me.' Even Mum was beginning to wonder about Sam's apparent charming exterior. But the decision about moving in with him was obviously mine to make.

Wednesday, 13 February 1991
Still no contact between us. I'm a bit depressed about it all. If I could get a job – get some money – get a life. If the lawyer would phone up and tell us we have to sign on such and such a date, then that would help me make up my mind. If only I knew if Sam still cared about me, sent a card or flowers, or just made some kind of contact. I miss him, but I'm so angry about the whole 'car incident' – he doesn't realise what a shock it's given me. I could walk away from him altogether now . . .

By the end of that week even David and Ryan were questioning Sam's absence, and I felt I had to find out how he felt about our situation, in light of his most recent rage at me. It was possible that he had changed his mind about buying the flat with me, and I had to clear the situation up and find out. It would be reasonable, I told myself, to be nervy and short tempered before making such a commitment as he was prepared to do. My driving mistake had possibly been the last straw for him after another hectic week. He probably regretted it all and felt that he just couldn't bring himself to explain his action to me. Perhaps I took his outburst too personally, I reasoned. I decided to visit him in his house and see if he was ready to listen to what I had to say.

He seemed surprised to see me at his door, but he swung it open wide for me to go inside. He stood fidgeting with his shirt cuffs while I stood in front of him, mentally preparing my speech.

'I was disgusted by your vicious display last weekend. Did you enjoy it?'

'No,' he answered quietly.

'The kids were terrified, you ruined an entire weekend, and God only knows what you have in store regarding this flat we're supposed to be buying.'

'So you'll still move in with me?' he shot in, enthusiastic all of a sudden.

'Look, Susan,' he moved towards me with hands outstretched, 'things have been so bloody strained over the past few weeks, and I know I'm a bit on edge – I shouldn't have spoken to you like that, it was unforgivable . . .'

5 March 1991

Here at last! We got the keys yesterday, and I'm so happy, I just cannot believe we are here. The place seemed smaller than I remembered it, but Sam thinks it's about right for us. The boys are pleased with their bedroom and the fact that they'll be able to go out to play now. Sam has some time off, and we'll get started on some decorating, though not a lot needs done. We'll actually move in tomorrow – poor Ryan is getting a little uptight about leaving his Nana, whereas I think Mum is looking forward to the space she'll have, and the peace.

I feel so content here, I've finally decided on what I want and I think I've made the right choice for the children too. What a difference between moving into the wee flat I bought with Keith, and moving into this one. I think we'll be happy here . . .

David and Ryan soon began to feel comfortable in their new home and Mum came to visit as often as possible, after repeat requests from Ryan. He missed his Nana terribly, and Sam and I did all we could to comfort him. He carried on attending nursery, while David went to primary school looking smart in his new uniform. Sam continued to show an interest in David's school work, and insisted on driving him the short journey to school every morning before going to work. He also took on the responsibility of taking Ryan to his speech therapy visits every week. He fought in their corner for them if they were being picked upon by other children, and would brag about their milestones and achievements as if they were his own flesh and blood. I expected nothing less from him, and encouraged his relationship with them to continue.

My search for work continued, and I was at an interview nearly every week, which was some achievement considering the unemployment situation. I enjoyed my time during the day in the flat. I felt content and happy to do the housework and make sure everything was right for Sam. He seemed happy to be home after work and had time for the boys before helping them off to their beds.

I noticed that subtle changes were taking place, however. Sam took advantage of the area's pub scene and set about sampling nearly every hostelry until he found one which suited him. He did this on his own, despite Mum's constant assurances that she would babysit at anytime. He would go down to the pub perhaps twice a week and all Saturday afternoon. Our nights out were suddenly halted. There were no more surprise cards, or bouquets of flowers. Mother's Day came and went, with only a cursory apology, which prompted the children to set about creating their own artwork for me as a present, which was much appreciated.

Sunday, 31 March 1991
Ryan is going through one of his phases. His little character is changing again, and he is very determined in a kind of 'I want things my way, or else'. It always takes me a wee while to adjust to these changes. For a while it was David asserting himself, testing Mummy's reaction, now Ryan is at the forefront. It's only natural I suppose, all part of their growing up. Sam hasn't been too tolerant of them recently, though, and it's been a hard day with both boys in 'moaning moods' and I was almost pleased when Sam stomped off to his bedroom (like another wee boy) after he'd had enough. He's been there since, probably reading and enjoying the peace, while I cope with the children. Wish I could get a job.

Once the children were tucked up in bed for the night, I approached Sam who was lying full length on top of our bed. He was reading. 'Are you coming through now? I've made a cup of coffee,' I ventured, standing at the bottom of our bed. He turned a page without even looking at me and continued to read. I stood and merely watched him for a moment, which prompted him to raise his book so that now I couldn't actually see his face. I pressed my lips firmly together to stop myself blurting out a string of insults at him, and turned to leave the room. That night, my mind fully occupied by his ridiculous behaviour, I decided to sleep on the couch.

The following morning I awoke to giggles and muffled shouts which were filtering through from David and Ryan's bedroom. I immediately remembered the situation and hoped that Sam's attitude had changed. I got up and padded quietly through to our bedroom. He was awake and reading. I slipped gratefully beneath the quilt and shivered out loud for his benefit. I lay silently, looking at the side of his face. I imagined him turning towards me, saying he was so sorry, and holding me warmly. What a lovely way to start the day. At last he closed his book and placed it on the bedside table. He threw back his side of the quilt and rose to thump through to the bathroom.

I lay alone, warm in that enormous bed, running over and over the events of the day before in my head until it ached. We had all been seated at the table, Sam had made a beautiful lasagne that we were all keen to demolish. Ryan had done something (I hadn't seen anything) and Sam had roared at the top of his voice at the child.

'Jesus Sam, we all jumped the height of ourselves – no need to shout like that!' I had announced, with both hands placed dramatically over my heart. He had simply got up, left his untouched plate before him, and gone through to the bedroom. That was it.

> 8 April 1991
>
> Two days later, and he hasn't said one word to me. Can you believe it? I still don't even know what I'm supposed to have done! I've shouted at him, pleaded with him to tell me. I even whipped the quilt off him this morning, just to see if I could get a swear word out of him. Oh, he still talks to the boys, but he just doesn't answer me if I ask him anything or say something. It's awful this. What is he playing at?

The evening of my last entry, anxiously scribbled into my diary, saw a changed man entering the living-room. He put down his briefcase and approached me, holding me tight in his arms. Feelings of utter relief swept over me, whatever it was, was now over. He loved me again, and was kissing me, and saying he was sorry. He had rescued me from the wilderness I felt I was abandoned in when he had blatantly ignored me.

We talked late into the night and I explained my feelings that I had experienced during the past three days.

'I felt so angry when you told me off like that in front of the kids,' he explained. 'I felt like one of your little boys – it was a bit humiliating.'

'But I won't support you in screaming at any of the kids like that, Sam. What did you want me to do?'

'I don't know. I saw him screwing up his face when you put down his plate, and I told him to behave himself . . .'

'So that was it?' I had finally found out the actual reason for all this misery. 'Ryan made a face, and you bawled at him for that?

Christ, there is no way I would've backed you up against him. And that was why you totally ignored me like that, was it?'

'Well, once I'd calmed down a bit, well, I did feel I'd made a fuss over nothing, but, well, sometimes I just don't know how to end it, you know, how to apologise.'

'But, I stood there, and gave you ample opportunity to make up, and you flatly refused to even answer me. This went on for three days, Sam, not just three hours.' I was beginning to get angry at his insistence that he was right to behave like that.

For some days after that incident I continued to think about it. I didn't discuss it with anyone, no one would have believed me anyway, and Mum was busy arranging an exchange of houses so that she could move into a smaller, one-bedroomed flat. It was a fuss over nothing, and it was all over anyway.

For months after that life seemed settled and happy. We still enjoyed having our little house, which I kept clean and tidy during the week. We both looked forward to the weekends when we could drive out somewhere in the country for picnics and walks with the kids during the summer months. There was no hint of irritation or even unhappiness from Sam and he enjoyed the loose routine we had fallen into on Saturdays and Sundays. One of us would lie in bed for an extra hour or two, while the other got up with the boys to get their breakfasts and dress them. Sam would help with the shopping and would prepare Saturday's evening meal before getting washed and dressed to go to the pub in the afternoon. He would come home around seven or eight and spend the evening with his family. We would take turns in deciding on Sunday's main meal and Sam enjoyed trying out new recipes, and even tried his hand at baking. Since all of the housework was done by me during the week, there was little for him to do at the weekends, but he hardly ever refused to take his turn of the washing-up or hanging out the washing if I ever asked.

'I think it's lovely to see your man hanging out the washing like that, you know, my man wouldn't be seen dead with a washing basket on his hip like Sam does,' one of the neighbours commented one day. She had admired him from afar, she admitted. 'He is so sweet with those boys, you've been so lucky in finding a man like him, Susan.' I agreed happily.

David was now six years old and Ryan four. They loved Sam now and called him 'Dad', which pleased us both. Despite both lads being almost the same height, with similar colouring, they were very different in personality. David was still a bit of a loner, preferring to paint or sketch his time away from school. He day-dreamed his way through his lessons and would sit for hours in front of the television watching endless cartoons if we let him. Ryan continued to be the physical one. He loved playing football and rounders and was by far the more sociable of the two lads. They admired and boasted about their Dad to others and were well-liked by friends and neighbours who regarded them both as polite and well-behaved children. David wanted to be like Sam, and would even refuse the same foods that Sam disliked. Ryan, however, remained totally loyal towards me, preferring my opinion over Sam's and usually obeying my instructions over his Dad's too. Sam admitted to me how this annoyed him, and I was surprised that he should even spend time thinking about it.

'It certainly doesn't bother me that David thinks you are the sunshine of his entire world. It is possible that my character suits Ryan more than yours, or, it could be that I am his beloved old Mum.' I joked with Sam on the subject, but it bothered him.

At last I got a job as a part-time office clerk in a small office in Leith. It was a lonesome job, no one to talk to except customers on the phone and suppliers. It was off the beaten track, so despite my being the 'receptionist' there were no members of the public wandering in to break the day's monotony. I enjoyed the job more when it was pay day and felt good about my contribution towards the family's finances. We found ourselves discussing our future one evening, and we talked about getting married. Sam had never officially asked me to marry him, and I had never expressed any wish to have another husband. At that point in our lives though, with things running along so smoothly, we made plans for a small wedding in September. I was due a tax rebate, which I had decided to save for the wedding, and I started to save as much money from my wages as possible to go towards it. We decided on a register office affair, in Edinburgh city, with Mhari and Graham as our witnesses. Sam insisted that his mother be present also, and I secretly worried about the strain on her general health.

Marjery considered it a hard day's work if she had to get up to answer the front door more than once. She never walked anywhere, nor stood for longer than five minutes at any one time. However, Sam was adamant that she should be brought down to

Edinburgh early in the morning to spend the entire wedding with us, and I appreciated his need for his mother's approval. I organised everything and curbed as much expense as possible. I made the bouquets for myself and Mhari, bought my wedding suit in a sale and altered it to fit. The boys wore simple dress trousers and striped shirts and little ties that had elastic loops, so that they could be placed over their heads, already knotted neatly. They loved stretching them down to their knees, and laughed uncontrollably when the ties were snapped back up to their necks.

When the time came for our small party of guests to file out quietly to get into their respective taxis I took the opportunity of standing in front of the mirror for one last look at myself. This time I knew that I loved the man I was about to marry. Our teething troubles were over, it had been months since Sam had last gone silent. We had our beautiful home, and two healthy children who both loved their step-father. We were both mature adults, now taking the small step from just living together, to getting married. As we stood together, smiling endlessly for photographs, I promised myself that this marriage would be my last.

CHAPTER FIVE

'Don't fuckin' believe this . . .' he muttered as he pushed the contents of the drawer around frantically. I was instantly awake. 'Is it too much to ask you to pair my bloody socks properly?' he snarled. 'Look at this!' He turned to throw them in my direction.

Only two minutes earlier he had been caressing me lovingly, enjoying a few precious minutes in a sleepy embrace before rising for work. Now his eyes flashed with rage. I immediately sat up to examine the socks. Same shade, same pattern, same length. I checked them over again before answering him.

'But they are the same,' I ventured timidly, looking up at him. His face was already red. He dived across the room and snatched up the socks, holding them in front of my face.

'Aye, well, you're wrong – look, there are different patterns down the sides. Can't even pair my fucking socks right – no, no Susan, don't you move hen, I'll look for the other one just you lie there,' he spat viciously.

Turning back to the drawer, he pulled it out with such force that it shot off it's runners and fell to the floor.

I jumped up and hurried through to the linen cupboard where I hung our smaller items to dry. I grabbed a handful of his socks and, on return to the bedroom, I threw them at him. They fell gracefully around him, dotting the carpet at his feet. 'You're screaming at me because of that?' I roared, 'Jesus, you should be glad you've got someone to bloody wash and put them away – you should be thanking me not ripping my fucking head off . . . !' I already knew what was happening, and I knew what would happen next. This was it, his usual pattern. This time though my anger more than matched his.

I threw myself into my clothes while he continued to dress in silence, but his gaze never left me as I furiously ranted on.

'Everything gets done for you, everything. Christ, I'm surprised you didn't tell me to come and wipe your arse for you just then! But, oh . . . when the socks are paired up willy nilly like that well, we'd better call the *Evening News*, eh? Wait till the boys in the office hear this, Jesus, they'll be telling you to get a divorce, Sam . . . a crime like that?'

I was beyond myself with fury and I could see his face darkening. The boys ate their breakfast without comment, while I thumped around the kitchen completing chores at break-neck speed. My mind was overtaken, repeating the same explosive scene over and over.

'There's something wrong with you,' he suddenly announced on his way through from the hall. He jabbed a fat finger into the air speaking in a clipped controlled manner. 'I only asked you where my other sock was, and you react like that? You're a fuckin' mental case.' He pulled at the collar of his coat, while I met his hateful stare. 'You get yourself sorted out before I get back – or else,' he said, and he was gone.

And so it was, for the following fortnight. It was as if he lived in another world with no wife or family. He wouldn't answer a question or acknowledge a greeting or goodbye. He would sit alone at the table eating the dinner that I had prepared, usually rising to empty most of it into the bucket before retiring to our bedroom for the evening to read a book. There was no eye contact either, he wouldn't even look at me. He ignored David and Ryan, which was a new development. I was both heartbroken and infuriated at him including them in the argument. He acted as if they had never spoken.

Ryan gauged the situation as soon as he witnessed David standing patiently waiting for his Dad to look at a picture he had painted at school. Sam merely continued to stare at the television until I could stand it no longer and gently drew the lad away.

'Why's Dad not speaking to us?' Ryan asked me later.

'He's angry with Mum.'

'Not speaking to him then,' he announced. Constant rejection soon taught David not to approach Sam at all.

Again I felt hurt and angry at his punishment. I no longer begged him to talk with me (as I had sometimes done in the past) and I tried to concentrate on the children, trying to make up for their Dad's ignorance. When the boys went to bed, I sat alone in the living-room feeling tearful and despondent. I ached for him to come through to comfort me like a child waiting for reassurance after being told off. I felt so low that I barely scraped through each day, but felt adamant that I wouldn't be the one to patch things up as usual. I slept on the couch every night.

Mum was the only one I could confide in. She was disgusted at his behaviour towards her grandsons.

'He wants me to apologise . . . ' I explained.

'For not pairing his socks correctly?' she interrupted impatiently, 'I should bloody well hope not! When is he going to start acting his age, for God's sake? Bloody tantrums over his socks, well he obviously wants you to be as miserable as he is, the idiot, and if it was me I'd pretend I didn't have a care in the world. If he sees you enjoying yourself with the kids, he'll soon see that he's missing out. It's worth a try,' she added. 'And . . . ' she pressed my arm for effect, 'when he does decide to talk again, tell him to get to a bloody psychiatrist. Typical bloody man that – trying to make out that you're the one with the problem.'

Saturday, 8 February 1992

Sometimes I think I'm going mad, just like he told me I was. I hate this. Could understand this reaction to me shagging the next door neighbour, or gambling the housekeeping away – but socks! It's been a week so far. Should I remain unconcerned and unaffected? Or should I badger him until he says something (anything)? I reckon he must feel inferior in this relationship. Feels he must have me under his thumb. It's not enough that I want to do these things for him, that I love him and want to make life easier for him. It has to be that he's told me to do them. But, I can't just sit down and agree with him about how inadequate he obviously thinks I am. I *am* a good housewife. Luckily for him I am naturally tidy. I make sure all his clothes for the office are neatly pressed and hung in the wardrobe. He never has to wash up, make a bed or even lift a black bag out to the buckets. That's my job, according to him. And do you know what? I do it willingly. I do it because I want to take the hassle away from him. He can get up, get shaved, dressed and go to work concentrating fully on the day ahead. But, should I trip up and not do my job properly . . . well then, I should expect to be punished for it. God this is hard. Sometimes I want to scream into his face how much I hate this. And when he holds me close beside him in the morning, telling me how much he loves me, I think I'll burst with happiness . . .

During the second week of my punishment, I stopped making his evening meal and continued to sleep on the couch. Numbly I became resigned to my punishment. I raided the shelves at the library, looking for books about psychology. The family health section didn't have any titles entitled 'What To Do When Your Husband Won't Speak To You', so I thumbed my way through academic titles. I actually enjoyed reading them, but chapters were bare of facts about problems like Sam's.

I continued to reassure the boys whose first question on returning from school included an update on the situation.

'What's for eating and are you and Dad still arguing?'

'Yes. Dad is still not talking to Mum.' I offered the compulsory biscuit. 'Don't worry about it.'

'Will we move back to Nana's if you don't love Dad any more?' Ryan asked.

'Would you mind if we moved out?' I looked into his serious little face.

'No . . . but Dad would be all on his own then, eh?'

'Well, if you want someone to stay with you, you don't treat them like this, do you?' He shook his head and bit into his biscuit while heading towards the television.

The thought that the boys did not regard our home with Sam as permanent pricked me somewhat. That they automatically assumed if things got rough, Mum would simply move back to Nana's was a reasonable solution for any child their age. I had considered it too.

I was absolutely miserable, thanks to my loving husband, yet I felt powerless about the situation. Leaving would be one solution. But as I licked a sugared teaspoon I knew that I would only leave Sam once. There would be no point in all the upheaval, if I believed him – just one more time – and decided to move back in again.

Monday 17 February 1992
BASTARD. I hate this. I can't see any effect with what I'm doing.

I'm so bloody depressed but you'd think I was the happiest wife in the world when Sam and the kids are around. I wait till they're in bed before bursting into tears at the end of another lonely day. I joined a Woman's Group at the Community Centre today, just to hear someone talking to me! It's pathetic. I feel pathetic.

Just as well he loves me, eh? I want to hurt him too. I want to hit him, to bring his hi-fi down on his fat head. I want to fill up the basin and throw freezing water over him as he lies reading his endless bloody books.

I want to pelt his CDs at him as he walks through the door, to see him on his knees, crying and pleading with me to comfort him. To tell him it's okay – that everything will be all right now.

I was job hunting again after resigning at work. This meant I had little else to focus on throughout the day. My boss had suggested that my hours be converted to full time. The job itself was easy to do, simple clerical administration, a bit of typing and answering the phone. Unfortunately, there were long periods of inactivity within the trade when my days became long and tedious. I started to dread going into work only to sit and read or rearrange the filing cabinet, yet again. I promptly resigned when the prospect of facing the job for eight hours arose. I didn't even consider consulting Sam about it beforehand.

We desperately needed the money, however, so finding another job became a priority. Despite spending my entire wages on the housekeeping, money was becoming ridiculously tight. It was the issue Sam and I quarrelled most about. Although he received a reasonable salary as a sales rep, we were handicapped by paying off bills that he had run up months before we had met.

I kept a simple accounts system which helped me to budget his wage every month, whereas Sam would simply continue withdrawing money from the cash machine without a second thought to the consequences. Sometimes he would force our account into the red by pushing us over the official overdraft limit.

This would create a steady stream of letters from our bank informing us that we owed them another £15.

I dreaded opening the statements and adding up the cheques that had been written by Sam. His work expenses were usually spent on the first week he received them. Thereafter, he would withdraw money from our account to pay for petrol. Then he would suggest a family day out somewhere and get annoyed when I bluntly refused. 'It's only money for Christ's sake. You're so bloody paranoid,' he'd say.

While I viewed the £40 left in our account as essential money for day-to-day living during the following fortnight, Sam looked upon it as £30 to spend on a visit to the Safari Park complete with bought lunch and treats for the boys. This left me with £10 to buy daily milk and bread, papers and other incidentals for the next two long weeks. 'Of course, if you don't like the way I handle the money then get a job,' he'd return smartly when it became too complicated for him. This remark usually worked and I would leave the matter simmering gently on the back burner.

One night during the second week I decided to try once more. With no particular plan in mind I approached him as he sat up in bed reading. His book resting on his chest rose and fell with his breathing. 'It's been nearly two weeks, Sam. Two weeks without you even looking at me, let alone speaking.' Silence. 'What do you want me to do?' I asked calmly. I wanted to scream at him, my heart seemed to be beating in my throat. Silence. I moved around the bed towards him, perching on the edge of the duvet and placed a hand on his. He drew it away. I sighed and gently bent down onto my knees looking up at the side of his face. 'Sam, I am truly sorry for not pairing your socks properly. I promise never, ever to do it again,' my voice began to break because the words were sticking in my throat. They sounded ridiculous as I was saying them, but I forced myself to repeat the apology.

He turned to look at me and my act of pathetic humbleness. It went against everything that I had ever thought about myself. I felt that he had actually broken me. 'Psychiatrist couldn't help you then, eh?' he said, quietly, feigning sympathy as he turned back to the book.

Monday, 24 February 1992
Well, it worked! It was awful, painful and degrading and some would say stupid. But, it worked. He couldn't handle it to begin with. After I had returned to the living-room he went out, to the pub no doubt. Then the following evening he approached me while I sat alone watching television.

He still was not to blame of course. I shouldn't have stopped making his tea or slept on the couch. He said he felt embarrassed at my 'hysterical performance' the other night, oh, and if I hadn't paired his socks wrong, well, none of this would have ever happened, would it? I nodded gratefully, glad it was over. His apologies (for not talking) and assurances of undying love did little to ease my pain. I continued to sleep on the couch for several days after. Even now I find it hard to believe how far he took it this time. I can't trust the man. Not now.

At the woman's group the tutor would invite guests along to speak about their charity or line of work. One week a woman called Annie from Edinburgh Woman's Aid arrived to give a talk about the organisation. She explained the various forms of abuse that they dealt with, as well as violence. The group, six women in total, sat expectantly, holding warm coffee cups and snacking on biscuits for breakfast.

'A man might prevent his partner from leaving the house without him, keeping her so short of money that she can't buy anything until he gets home from work. He'll stop her having friends maybe by behaving rudely in front of them or by doing something that frightens them away from keeping in touch. Her family might even be barred from his house, which means she is isolated and can't tell anyone about just what is happening at home. The list goes on and is easily explained if anyone does confront him about how he treats his partner.'

Annie then asked for questions from the group while women shifted uneasily in their seats. I found the subject fascinating. 'So why doesn't the wife leave her man if he does that to her?' This was the question we all wanted to ask.

'Imagine it's tomorrow morning and you have to leave the house suddenly – so suddenly that you don't have time to get dressed even . . . what would you do and where would you go?' She directed the question to us all with a sweep of her arm.

'I'd phone my Mum, and ask her to come and get me,' suggested Sharon.

'You can't. Your man is standing by the phone with one of his shoes in his hand. He's chasing you around the sitting-room and the kids are screaming.'

Annie was painting the scenario with dramatic commentary.

'Run for the door – try to get out, take the kids with me,' Moira blurted out.

'Okay, let's say you get out with the kids, but you're in your nightie and the children have no shoes on. Where would you go?'

'Knock on a neighbour's door . . .' Leeanne offered. 'No, no, I wouldn't. He'd follow me. They might not be in,' she concluded, as if talking to herself.

'So you are outside and running away from him. Where now?' Annie pressed.

'I'd still go to Mum's house,' I ventured. 'I could get there before he did.'

'So you know he's behind you, he's trying to stop you from getting there and spilling the beans about what's happening at home. Would she be in?'

'Yes.'

'But you'd be stuck in her house, possibly all day, when would you go home?'

'I'd send my brother round to him,' shot in Sharon.

'Get the police, that would shame the bastard!' someone added. Everyone was throwing in their own versions of what should happen next when Annie raised her hands for quiet.

'Right ladies, let's go back a step and imagine he has assaulted you and left the house. You've managed to pack the kids off to school anyway, and you're now sitting alone in the house thinking about it. What would you do?'

'Pack my bags and leave before he gets home,' stated Linda, which prompted several nodding heads to agree.

'I'd go to my sister in Broomhouse, her husband is bigger than mine.'

'So you'd go to stay with her. Does she have kids?'

'Yes, three.'

'Do you have money?'

'A wee bit.'

'Would you take the kids out of school to go to Broomhouse Primary or would you leave them with your husband?'

'Well . . .'

'Would you get a job, and who would look after the children? Where would you live or will you stay on at your sister's forever?'

Linda gave up, Annie had made her point.

'You'd have to cope with immediate danger to yourself, and

possibly the children, deal with day-to-day living while pretending that nothing is out of the ordinary to family and friends. Then, on top of that you have to find the time and confidence to arrange alternative accommodation, money, changing schools and facing the prospect of your man following you with either promises of big changes in the future or with threats of violence if you don't return to him.'

The consequences seemed overwhelming. The group continued to discuss the issue long after Annie's departure and we agreed that women in that situation were to be applauded not criticised.

When I told Sam about what I'd learnt that day, he tutted with equal disgust at each shocking tale. He certainly didn't consider himself as an abusive husband.

> 5 April 1992
> . . . I found it so hard to relate to. I think I would definitely leave if Sam battered me like that. Even better, I'd get him to move out. She never mentioned anything about men refusing to communicate. I'm so glad Sam doesn't keep me short of money and doesn't vet my friends. He practically forces me to go out with pals. Annie said that when a woman leaves her man for good, it's usually when they realise that he doesn't love her any more! As long as she thinks he still loves her – she'll put up with it. God. Just hope it never happens to me . . .

As 1992 wore on, Sam's rages and mind-crushing silences continued at a rate of nearly one a month. Although I continued to scribble down my feelings of pain and utter desperation, once they were resolved I had the ability to forget them. Only when yet another upset occurred would I compare it to a previous humiliation.

Instead of looking outside for help, I turned inwards believing that only I could solve our problems. I set about making everything as perfect as possible. I took serious note of little preferences he'd point out to me and small annoyances that could explode into terrifying rages.

I became even more house proud, and the flat was immaculate with everything in its place. The meals were varied despite the inadequate budget and they were planned to the minute when his sleek grey Sierra rolled into the estate every evening.

I decided to register as a childminder, attending all the preliminary meetings that were required. I badgered the social work office for a start date for my new business, anxious to make some much-needed cash. When I did start minding my first charge I felt I could tackle substantially the overdraft once more.

In the beginning I told Mum that we'd had another row and another one. But most times I didn't, preferring to forget the unpleasant side of my marriage rather than talk it all over again with someone else. As a result Mum was sometimes lulled into a false understanding of my life with Sam. I still felt immensely proud of our situation. The fact that my husband worked diligently and we had bought a house actually meant something to me – it represented some kind of achievement for us. Our children were happy, healthy and nothing but a credit to us. I was eager to carry on with the illusion and still looked forward to our future with optimism.

Sam's willingness to throw a rage in front of David and Ryan was becoming more apparent as time progressed. It was a strategy that served him well. I'd agree to anything without objection as long as he didn't scream and create chaos in the boys' presence.

He began to throw things around the room, upsetting piles of books or washing during a rage. His height and size meant that regardless of where you were in the living-room, he was beside you having a tantrum.

The boys would cry pathetically, making sure that they were standing or sitting somewhere together for comfort. Comfort that I couldn't give them. Drawing Sam's attention to their distress altered nothing. Eventually, they learnt to clear out as soon as an irate mutter left his mouth. David would leave immediately – Ryan would hang back anxiously watching events, until one of us shut the door on him. The only way that I could protect them from such frightening scenes was to try to keep them away from their Dad altogether. This was an impossibility.

Once we were all in the car, Sam driving us somewhere. He suddenly objected to something I said and slammed his foot onto the brakes, catapulting us all forward in our seats. I learnt quickly not to discuss anything even remotely important while he was in control of the car. Every time he accelerated the speed, or screeched to a halt to shut me up, he drove the boys to near hysterics. More and more I found I had to restrain myself from speaking out against any of his actions whereas Sam never held back. I controlled myself – and he controlled me too.

When he began to throw things around the room the house resembled a battle zone. Inevitably he started to throw things at me – tins of soup, shoes, brushes and any books that lay about. Thin plaster walls soon became dented by the objects that had missed their mark.

When all these incidents ended, Sam would return to the loving, thoughtful and caring man that he always portrayed to the outside world. He had time to play with David and Ryan, enjoying their company and openly telling them how he loved them.

During a shouting match one day, he slapped me soundly across the face. The palm of his hand covered my left ear and my hearing immediately altered. I angrily lashed back with a 'do or die mentality', kicking and pulling at him. The boys screamed, both scrambling for the door. I managed to pull Sam's glasses off and threw them across the room hoping to buy myself enough time to reach the door without him. It worked, and outside the boys stood crying pitifully.

Sam cleared out quickly, allowing us time to sit together amongst the debris, recovering from the ordeal. That week I visited the doctor about my hearing. I lied, telling her I had been play wrestling with one of the boys when it happened. She nodded sympathetically and without further question.

After his regulation week's silence, and his apology for hitting me, Sam flatly refused to believe that he had actually burst my eardrum. He remained adamant that I'd simply added the injury to my list for effect.

Later rages saw him pushing and dragging me around the flat. His superior strength meant little effort on his part to damage me – I just had to knock against something for it to hurt like hell. His post mortem excuses were as predictable as any party's answer on policy. 'It's the way you keep screeching at me, it winds me up,' he explained once.

'Oh, so you want me to remain silent while you punch me around the room then?'

'I never punched you.'

'Okay, when you slap me, push me, pull me . . .'

'I only pushed you because you were trying to hit me back. You tried to kick me!' he pointed out petulantly.

'So I'm not allowed to defend myself, or fight back. I'm supposed to stand there quietly and let you batter me to the ground . . !'

'No . . . of course not . . . I don't know, I don't know.'

I never held back in telling him how much each rage damaged me, our love and, of course, the children. I spelt out my feelings of humiliation, powerlessness, rejection and utter confusion. Every detail was explained over and over again with him when I knew he just wanted to forget all about it.

Remarkably, even then, despite my telling Sam how hard I was finding life with him, I never suggested that he leave. Nor did I threaten to go elsewhere with the boys. I soldiered on, rallying him with an optimistic speech telling him that we could beat any problem as a couple as long as we were both willing to keep on trying. And I still was.

CHAPTER SIX

In July 1993 we celebrated the birth of our beautiful daughter, Rosie. We had moved from the flat in Leith to a large family house in West Lothian. It was my dream home and I knew as soon as we entered to view it that we would live there. An ex-council house, it boasted three double bedrooms with fitted carpets and blinds. The main bedroom had a luxurious cream-coloured deep pile carpet, large fitted wardrobes and four modern concealed lights in the ceiling connected to a dimmer switch. The boys' bedroom was much bigger than the claustrophobic little cupboard they had in Leith, and even the baby's room had clean white fitted wardrobes. The kitchen had been extended by the previous owners, with new units from floor to ceiling.

The living-room seemed barn-like, with one entire wall being taken up by new patio doors with expensive vertical blinds. The upstairs bathroom had just been revamped, the owner assured us, with a pale peach suite which included a bidet. The large garden was only partly grassed and looked overgrown. The patio seemed green tinged, the brick barbecue rusty and covered with leaves. I loved every feature, even the garage. To buy one in similar condition in Edinburgh would have been financially out of the question for us.

During the week we were moving in, Sam and I walked the short distance to the boys' new primary school. They seemed anxious about it, and we assured them that this would be their last school change. After all, the house we had just bought was so big that we'd never have to move again.

Sam had been promoted yet again, this time to office manager. This boosted his ego and meant a welcome increase in salary. We also kept the same company car, which was more important to us now that we lived in the country but it also meant an increase in his stress levels. He would leave the house at 7 a.m. to avoid the traffic and get home about 7 p.m. every night.

For two or three months following the previous year's set-to, Sam and life in general became calm and somewhat reassuring. He had not resorted to violence again and any upsets after that had fizzled out successfully, with no harm being done to anyone. This gave us time to consider starting a family. We discussed the issue sensibly, considering the effects a child between us would have on David and Ryan. Sam's promotion was a financial help to us and, of course, my ability to find children to mind after I'd had the baby. I was keen to have another baby. I looked forward to enjoying time with possibly my last child as an 'at home wife and mother'. I had never had that luxury with the boys, since I was mostly working throughout their toddler years. Despite Sam's already blighted history with my own sons, I had no doubts that he would be anything other than an excellent father. I wanted to give him a child of his own and imagined the added responsibility would be one that he was more than able to share.

The nine months that I had been pregnant were the most peaceful and loving times we had as a family. Sam was thrilled and almost childlike with excitement when we realised I was pregnant. He followed every step of the pregnancy, always considerate of my needs. He educated the boys, who were both looking forward to their new sister/brother, and included them in any preparations for the birth. 'I don't want the boys to be called half-brothers when the baby comes,' he said one night as we lay talking in bed. 'And I think we should seriously consider changing the boys' name to Brown, otherwise they might feel left out of the family.' David and Ryan still had their birth names and we decided to change their last name to ours.

There were few pubs in our area and none within walking distance so Sam's weekly nights out were suddenly stopped. He bought in cans from the supermarket and preferred to drink at home. This meant long, loving nights together watching the television with the occasional evening out together, while Mum babysat the boys. Mum and Marjery, both suitably pleased about the new grandchild, set about knitting various outfits and pram covers for the baby. Marjery never forgot to include the boys whenever she bought something towards the baby, and now considered them her own grandsons.

At last I thought we had ridden the storms. Mum travelled out twice a week to visit us. The journey involved catching two buses, taking one and a half hours, sometimes longer if she missed a connection. I missed Mum a lot since I was isolated in my new house. I had no friends beside me, except for one who lived with her two children in another village. My neighbours were middle aged with grown-up families who lived elsewhere. Eventually, Mum applied to be transferred out to our area and was put in touch with a gentleman who desperately wanted to move back into Edinburgh. The two quickly viewed each other's houses, Mum's tenement, and his modern cottage-style terraced house. The deal was made and the exchange of houses went through without a hitch. This meant Mum had moved out to be beside us with barely two weeks to go before the baby was due. We had missed each other's company in the months we had lived so far away and the boys were eager to have their beloved Nana only a bike ride away once more.

Again, I had been lucky in experiencing another trouble-free and healthy pregnancy. I hardly gained weight and was able to wear my own normal clothes. This meant I avoided buying maternity clothes.

Monday, 19 July 1993

. . . I had to be told twice that she was a girl – I was so sure it would be another boy. Sam was stunned into tearful silence as he saw her for the first time. So relieved she was okay and the birth was so quick and clean etc. Mum and Marjery were thrilled, Mum brought the boys up to the ward to see her – they were fascinated by her. Apart from the odd day, I haven't been engulfed by depression (I suffered from post-natal with Ryan). I've gone back to my normal weight and Sam has helped out so much during his two weeks off work. We named her Rosie.

David and Ryan are absolutely besotted with their little sister. Ryan walks into the room with his lips permanently puckered, ready to kiss her. David has the knack of soothing her to sleep in his arms. Still haven't got used to the novelty of having pink frilly things to put her in. I'm so used to blue.

Time is so taken up with the boys being on holiday and Rosie that this is the first time I've been able to scribble something down. I'm so glad that she is here, and everything is fine with her. I'm so happy.

When Sam returned, reluctantly, to work I carried on my normal tasks, and more, while dealing with the new baby. I immediately began advertising my vacancies for childminding. In an attempt to reduce Sam's stress levels I now looked after the finances but it annoyed him that he no longer had control over the house purse-strings. I immediately set about paying the bills and putting aside money every month to bring down the dreaded overdraft. This meant little for extras and I concentrated on kitting out the children before ourselves.

Totally heartsick of having a permanently empty purse, I decided that drastic measures were needed. I phoned the pubs and hotels around the village to ask about gaining work as a part-time barmaid. I had previous experience and I soon found a job. I worked the busiest nights of the week, Friday and Saturday. Rosie was barely three months old and still waking for her 2 a.m. feed, but it was a sacrifice I was willing to make. Remarkably, Rosie slept right through to her 6 a.m. feed almost as soon as I started that job. It was as if she knew I needed the rest.

Tuesday, 19 October 1993
The boys are off for their autumn break, and so is Sam. He's back to his usual hateful, petty, childish self again. Motive? Apparently my face wasn't straight enough after a visit to his mother's yesterday. He thought I had something nasty to say about his Mum (I didn't) and slowly worked himself up into a tantrum. I looked as if I was calmly reading the evening paper – inside, I was totally destroyed at the thought of him returning to his bad old ways. He ripped up my paper as I was attempting to read it. When I didn't crawl up to him asking him 'What's wrong darling?' he decided to immobilise the car to stop me from taking the boys to see a film in Edinburgh! It seems that this holiday, Sam is ready for another big fight scene. This time I think I've had enough . . .

Suddenly, the idyllic previous 13 months was washed away in yet another rip tide of insults and threatening behaviour. I crumbled at the thought of it all starting again, and desperately tried to keep a leash on my emotions as his vicious comments filled the room and echoed inside my head.

'Please let me take the boys to the pictures Sam, I promised them this trip today – don't include them in all this.'

'I'm not stopping you from taking them anywhere.'

'Then what have you done to the car?'

'Haven't done anything to the car. Christ, take the bastards where- ever you like,' he snarled.

'What did you say? These are your sons you're insulting . . .'

'I didn't insult them.'

Sam's new found tactic in trying to convince me that my sanity was in question had the desired effect. His continual efforts crushed me into a lame silence. On that occasion, he even went to the extent of looking up the telephone directory muttering 'psychiatrists, psychiatrists' over and over. When I escaped the house that day (by bus) to trudge the streets of Edinburgh alone, he invited Mum up to the house for company.

When she asked where I was, he said that I was upset, but he didn't know why. He seemed anxious and perplexed about the situation. He claimed that I had refused to talk to him – and admitted to taking something out of the engine of the car. He said he did that in desperation, an attempt to get me to say something! Mum listened intently, expressing concern and surprise. She was well aware of her son-in-law's failings after three years. She knew her daughter, even better than he did.

He entertained her and the children all day in between cleaning the house and making lunch for everyone. He even explained carefully to David and Ryan, Mum told me later, that they would have to go to the cinema another day, since Mum had gone off somewhere without warning!

Later incidents saw him locking me out of the house by keeping his key inside the lock. We had an inner vestibule door with one key only. We never locked it while we were in the house, and only closed the door whenever we went out. Once, I had approached the front door expecting it to be locked against me. Relief covered me briefly when it opened easily, until I discovered that the inner vestibule door wouldn't open. It was after 9 p.m., the children were in bed. I wanted to take one of the stones from the rockery in the front garden and smash the glass with carefree abandon. But, I had to stand timidly tapping the glass, until my husband deemed it prudent to let me into my own house. Any suggestion that he had locked me out deliberately was hotly denied. He presented himself as a total innocent.

Once Sam had returned to his hurtful habits, I found myself with a changed attitude towards him. To me, it had been obvious that he could control his temper, that it wasn't some mystical brainstorm that would engulf him against his will. He had been a model husband and father for over 12 months, without a hint of his previous behaviour.

For whatever reason, it was clear that he had chosen to return to his former self. Entries in my diary became more bitter and less hopeful about our future.

Monday, 25 October 1993

It was lunchtime Friday before he lowered himself to speak to me. Apparently, he thinks I cannot be as upset as I make out. He thinks that when I cry, that it's just an act. That time he disabled the car, he said he didn't like the reaction he got from me afterwards. What bloody reaction did he expect?

He has agreed to me making an appointment for us at the Marriage Guidance Council. I remember trying that with Keith, although I don't know why. I think I had lost all respect for the man by the time we had turned up for the first appointment. Anyway, maybe they can point us in the right direction for some serious help for Sam and his stupid ways. Maybe they'll teach him to say something totally radical like 'Let's talk about this dear'. Huh. It'll never happen and I'll tell you why. Because the man is an idiot. A typical dunderheided, selfish, childish, dull-brained, inadequate fat bastard. And do you know the saddest part in all this? I married him!

The appointment at Edinburgh's Relate office was a disaster from start to finish. Sam was hyped up and anxious about the session despite my reassurances about what would be expected of him. He could not get his head around the idea of counselling. He thought it an opportunity for me to 'tell tales' on him, while he sat cowering and defenceless. He interrupted me endlessly, while I attempted to tell the woman counsellor what had happened so far. His voice was high pitched and strained. When I reached the part about Sam slapping me around the living-room – he almost lunged at the woman, forcing her to listen to his side.

'Aye, but, but . . . that was only a slap or two. What about her trying to kick me in the testicles after that, eh? She doesn't tell you about that!' He sat back, folding his arms in a self-satisfied manner.

'I think your wife has adequately covered both sides of the story so far, Mr Brown – perhaps you could let her finish filling me in and then we can all discuss things together,' she explained calmly, returning her gaze to me. I entertained the image of my administering a quick kick to his 'testicles' in order to shut him up and calm him down, but continued with my monologue. It was clear that I was wasting my time.

When we finally left, Sam bursting out onto the street like a caged animal, we discovered that the car had been towed away by the traffic police! Two hours later, and £125 lighter, we were driving west at a maniacal speed. Even the black night seemed a tinge lighter than Sam's mood, and I regretted ever suggesting the session at all. We thanked Mum for babysitting and I drove her home. Later that evening Sam spelt things out for me in a cool and firm manner.

'Look, Susan, there is no way I'm going to travel into Edinburgh every week just so that we can slag each other off like that. I'm quite happy with the way things are between us, and I try hard to make things better, I really do. I don't want our marriage to fail, and for me to be alone with debts again because of all the child support I'll have to pay, I mean it's just too much to lose. I'm determined to try harder to patch things up after a fight, but this counselling thing just isn't the way.'

Wednesday, 17 November 1993
At that point, I thought how little he cared about us. That if we did start to go under, I could still fight for us, but he certainly wouldn't. He said that he could never guarantee that he wouldn't go into another huff again, or that he would never be violent again. Great, eh? In other words, like it or lump it girl!

I felt like I wanted to die when he said all that. The sheer frustration and hopelessness I felt was overwhelming. The Child Support Agency wanting his money seemed the most important detail to him. I am 30 today, and I wish I'd never been

born. I got fuck all from my husband and family, oh I did receive
an apology – one of many I have received from him over the past
three years . . .

And so we stumbled on throughout the rest of the year. I was
looking after a couple of children, on a part-time basis, and it
meant that I could give up the gruelling hours at the pub every
weekend. My long tedious days were broken by visits to and from
Mum and my friend Kerry from Broxburn. At night, when Sam
came home to sit at the table and consider his dinner, he brought
with him the atmosphere that now suited us both. If he was
sending me to Coventry, the dinner went into the bucket and
he'd make his usual concoction of cheese sandwiches and strong
coffee. I was beyond caring about what he ate. I concentrated on
the children instead, but was ever watchful of Sam for any signs
that he would include the boys in one of his moods. As Rosie
grew up into curious babyhood and became more mobile, she
also demanded more attention – as nature intended. The boys
still adored her and considered her every need. It was lovely to
watch them together. She loved to be included in David's
imaginary play in the garden, and would crawl excitedly under
the sheet that he had erected as a makeshift Action Man tent for
them both. When she was close to walking, she would demand
they take her hands, while they walked her about the garden.
Ryan was Rosie's official entertainments manager, which
involved him pretending to trip up, falling on his face into the
grass, he would make funny noises that had her chuckling
appreciatively at his antics. He would smother her with kisses
while her fat little hands attempted to push him away, and then
she would yell for him to stay with her. when the boys pretended
to chase her, the ultimate game of excitement, she would
frantically crab-walk away from them, holding onto the furniture
until she reached Sam's knees from where she would scream in
sheer anticipation of them catching her.

11 June 1994
Here we go again.
    You can tell how nervy I am, by the state of my handwriting.
It started this time with the stair gate. Sam has his 'Nasty Head'
on today, and I'm about ready to rip it off his pathetic fat

shoulders! I'm not going to back down though. His mum phoned today and he took great delight in screaming at me while she was listening. How humiliating.

The following day, a Sunday, I prepared to take the children into Edinburgh Zoo. I'd saved precious pounds towards the trip knowing that Sam preferred to stay at home for a quiet day in. I had got up still resentful about the abuse he had spat at me while his mother had been on the telephone. I could hardly look at him, I felt so much disgust for the man, and I elected to sleep with the baby that night.

Sam came downstairs and into the living-room where I was sitting without even glancing at me. As Rosie was at the stage of trying to climb the stairs at every opportunity, I asked Sam to put the stair gate up, on his way through to the kitchen. He refused, and I tutted wearily before rising to do it myself. That was it. He charged through from the kitchen, his face already brightly coloured with anger.

'For Christ's sake I'm trying to get my breakfast here and I've got to carry out your fucking orders first. Would you like me to mow the lawn before I eat?' he screamed into my face. 'Perhaps I could make the beds for you while you sit on your arse, you lazy cow!'

Rosie was stunned into silence, but she made her way across the carpet towards me. Ryan sat rigid in his seat, looking at me and I nodded to him, almost psychically assuring him that I understood his fear. David promptly stood up and moved towards the open patio doors. He nervously tied his shoelaces on his trainers, his gaze never leaving the cartoons on the television. Meanwhile, I trembled with absolute fury. I knew the pattern. I recognised the build-up, and this was it. No matter what happened now, there was no going back. No matter what I said now or attempted to do, nothing would change his mood. No neighbours ever came to the door at the right time to save us, no phones ever rang with good news that placated him enough for me to think up some kind of diversion to his plan. Events had to take their course now, and we must be a part of them. My mind screamed out abuse at him. I hated him with a vengeance. But still I sat, seemingly subdued and becalmed.

'What time are you taking them to the zoo?' His voice was firm and he looked at me steadily, awaiting my answer.

'It depends. If you've disabled the car again, we'll be catching the bus within the hour. Other than that, we'll be out of your hair by 11 o'clock.' I returned his gaze, our eyes meeting in rare contact.

'What do you mean?'

'Oh, you know, Sam . . .' I placed Rosie down onto the couch beside me. 'Just presumed you'd like to drag the children into all of this – by denying them a trip into the zoo, and then blaming me for it.' The hair on the back of my arms and tenuous threads at the nape of my neck were bristling.

'Don't get fuckin' smart with me!'

I continued to stare at his face and the sweat that was shining on his forehead and the bridge of his nose. Normally, I would have done anything but look at him. I would have been in constant motion, carrying out little tasks, pretending to be busy and unconcerned. But I sat motionless and watched him turn back into the hallway, and into the kitchen. The sounds of cutlery and pots being thrown about clattered their way through to us, as the television blared out happy signature tunes heralding the start of another cartoon. He appeared once more at the doorway.

'Right arsehole, I'm taking them into Edinburgh. You can fucking clear up the mess in that bloody tip of a kitchen,' he snarled.

'Oh, great boys. Dad's going to entertain you today,' I announced cheerily. 'And if you want the kitchen tidied, *you* do it!'

When Marjery answered the phone, she couldn't hear anyone speaking. She could hear screaming, lots of screaming, and roaring and general crying in the background. She heard a child's voice screeching something, like, 'leave her, leave her!'. The thumping sounds were similar to what one would hear if someone had dropped the telephone, and she motioned to Lawrie her son to come over to listen in. Then the line went dead.

I thanked the day for being so glorious and still. The garden looked beautiful, and I spent the entire day outside, wrapped in thoughtful solitude. I went over and over that morning's events, trying desperately to think of other things. What else was there to think about I mused? This is my life.

When Sam eventually returned with the children, he immediately phoned his mother, unaware that she had actually heard that morning's beatings. The boys came out into the garden and both raised their arms to cuddle me gently. I tried hard not to cry, but held them tight, asking them if things had been okay at the zoo. They nodded in silence.

'Was it okay for me to stop him, Mum? I managed to kick him, and I held onto his arm – I think it stopped him,' Ryan said, and a visual snatch of him throwing his wiry seven-year-old little body at his hulk of a step-father flashed before me once more.

'Yes, it was okay.' It was all I could say. My throat felt tight with the grief that I felt for these boys, and what they had just been through.

'Don't tell me, tell *her*!' Sam was shouting. This was Marjery attempting to tell her 34-year-old son off, I mused. 'Thirty years too bloody late,' I scoffed inwardly. But at least she was trying. He started to detail my inadequacies, the state of the house, the untidy kitchen I was unwilling to clean; listing the reasons why he had to batter me around the living-room, trying to get her to see his point.

I checked Rosie, who was lying sleeping on the settee, where Sam had put her. She looked serene and so innocent. I picked up my bag and left the house, with Ryan following behind. We walked over to Mum's house without talking and I held his hand firmly. She seemed pleased to see us and asked where David and Rosie were.

'Rosie is having a snooze on the couch, David is out to play I think.'

'Dad punched Mum this morning. Twice.' Ryan glanced at me before continuing. 'He hit her with the phone . . .' He trailed off, but I made no attempt to stop him. Mum looked at me before carrying the cups of tea she had just made through to her sitting-room. Her lips were pursed and she folded her hands on her lap when she sat.

'Is this true Susan?'

'Yeah. He's done it before. Twice, maybe three times before.'

Ryan suddenly changed the subject and began burbling on about something at school. Neither of us was listening though. Mum reached out her hand towards the phone. She picked up the receiver and with the same hand pressed one digit, and held the handset up to her ear. Ryan and I watched mutely.

'If you *ever* lift a hand to my daughter again, I promise you this, my lad, I'll be in your house within five minutes – and I'll be leaving with your balls as *earrings*!' and she slammed down the handset. The phone rang immediately. 'You cowardly bastard!' she screamed, and slammed it down again.

'Was it him?' I asked.

'Yes.' And we laughed nervously at the scene that had just been played before us.

CHAPTER SEVEN

Sam left the house that afternoon, taking Rosie with him, while I was at Mum's with Ryan. He had dropped David off at her street with a letter Sam had written to his mother-in-law. In it, he admitted to hitting me – giving the reason why. He also added that since he had apologised to me afterwards, that there was no reason for her (mum) to phone him with 'childish insults'. Mum smartly ripped it up.

David told us that Sam had packed some nappies. We presumed he was heading home to his mother with the baby. I hoped desperately that this was the case. Anything was possible now, and his thirst for revenge knew no limits. When he arrived home early on Monday morning I lifted Rosie from him gratefully. He was calm and apologetic. Remorseful, all smiling, all agreeing, tearful and pathetic.

'Well, I'm getting out Sam. I've had it here.' I launched into my mentally prepared speech, ignoring his apologies. He stood motionless, his mouth slightly open.

'I've phoned Woman's Aid, they say they have a space for me and the kids, and I've an appointment with the doctor this morning.' This was only the second time I had told him that I was intending to leave, but the mention of relevant authorities sent him into a panic.

'Look hen, wait . . . Don't do anything rash just now.' I watched him scraping about for reasons why I should stay. 'Look, I'll go to work, I'll grab some things and I'll stay at Mum's for a couple of nights, eh? Give us some space. Don't go to the shelter though, just you stay here hen.'

'Okay. And when you are at Marjery's, think on this. There is precious little hope for us now, Sam. If I leave this house, it won't be because of what I say or do, or the kids, or the house or even my work and yours. Not even because of the constant bloody lack of money. It'll be because of you. *You*! Now, either you go to see a psychologist about *your* problem – or come back to an empty house.' He nodded enthusiastically, before heading upstairs to pack some clothes. I was too busy talking and caressing sweet Rosie in our garden to turn to say goodbye to him – and he just left. I had no feelings of victory after my speech. His willingness to please was the usual response to my threat of leaving. Little would change, I realised, until I actually got him to a psychologist, but I did feel determined to get him to see someone. It was after all, our last hope.

> Wednesday, 22 June 1994
> God, what is happening to me? I find it so hard just to live these days. Trying to cope with the last fortnight's events. We went to the doctor (in the hope that he would refer us somewhere else) and his advice was comical. He advised us, quite solemnly, not to fight. His theory, as he explained it to us carefully, was this: we fight over trivial things anyway, so why bother? He said to Sam, 'If you feel like slapping your wife again, just walk away.' There now, that's solved everything, now, off you both go and be happy families again! Unbelievable or what?

Sam was delighted with the GP's advice, and was making himself ready to leave the surgery. I stayed put, determined to get what I came for.

'Your advice is very sensible and seems the obvious approach in such a difficult situation, but with the greatest respect,' I lied, 'my husband and I have been attempting to do exactly as you suggested for the past four years.' He sat motionless and seemed to be hanging on my every word. 'It's because we can't do that, that we're here today. I was really hoping that you could put my husband forward for some kind of psychological counselling. Is there such a thing?'

'Oh yes, but unfortunately the waiting list runs into months. There's a lot of call for the service,' he replied. 'Mrs Brown, excuse me for asking this, but do you always talk like that?' He raised his eyebrows, waiting for an answer.

'Pardon?'

'Just listening to you explaining your situation, you know you have a very good command of language. You are a very articulate young woman,' he enthused.

'Mmmm,' I nodded politely while a quick glance at Sam's puzzled face confirmed my fears that the GP was straying off the subject somewhat.

'I suspect,' he continued, replacing the top on his biro and dropping it confidently onto his prescription pad, 'that during an argument you probably express yourself quite well, whereas Mr Brown . . .' he trailed off while we both looked at Sam moving uncomfortably in his chair.

'Aye. She can shout out five sentences, before I open my mouth sometimes!' he offered generously.

Encouraged by his theory being proved, he attempted to thrill us further. 'And you know when you feel yourselves getting into an argument, Mrs Brown, well, when Mr Brown here does decide to walk away, you will let him, won't you?' He looked hard into my face as my mind desperately tried to latch onto his train of thought.

'What I mean by that is, you won't say anything nasty . . . like "Oh, you're just a chicken, can't take a fight." You won't badger him into a fight, will you, Mrs Brown?'

It was all becoming clear now.

'No,' I answered resignedly, thinking 'God, if only you bloody knew just what happened, you sad bastard.' The obvious fact that Mr GP had decided that it must be me that asks to be battered around our home in front of our children had to be laid aside for the moment, while I struggled to obtain just what we'd gone to the surgery for.

'Would private insurance help at all?' I ventured. His eyes visibly widened at this question.

'You have private health insurance? Well, yes, yes of course it would!' he said, grabbing his pen and removing it's top. 'I could write off today to a clinic in Edinburgh that would be able to see you much sooner . . .' he gushed.

Despite an appointment to see a psychiatrist the following month, Sam was beginning to get cold feet as the day approached. When I offered to attend his appointment with him, he was visibly relieved.

'I suppose you think he'll be far more interested in me, eh?' I could practically see the thought racing around his empty little head.

'Well . . . you obviously play a part in all this, don't you? If it wasn't for you, I wouldn't hit you, would I?' And there it was. His opinion, still firmly set in concrete. If it wasn't for me. Said it all, really.

Friday, 24 June 1994.
This time last year I was about to give birth to Rosie. Such hope, such excitement. Sam was so loving, so anxious about everything. Not any more. I'm down and out just now. So depressed. Can't stop thinking about that last time he punched me. The hurt, the humiliation, just shouts at me all day. I cry when it gets bad, like there has been a death in the family. I get bloody flashbacks of it all, as if I haven't seen enough. I don't want my marriage to end, I still want what I've got. But I can't cope with Sam hitting me like that. Neither can the kids. Sometimes I think I can. I think, if it's only going to happen every five months or so, maybe I could cope. Other times, when I'm still aching two weeks after our last bout, I know that the next time must be the last and that my marriage must end. I think up ways to get out, running over in my head what I'll have to do. He doesn't believe he's bad enough to split us up – and, of course, it's all my fault. He'll stay in the house and I'll have to go with the kids. God, it's terrifying.

Now I know why Linda ran away – I remember how bewildered he was that she should run off like that. He'd done nothing and it was all her fault. I wish I could just fade away now. Now, before I have to leave this beautiful house and go to live in yet another council shit hole. I've lived in them all, it shouldn't be too hard for me to get used to it. Hope this psycho guy can help.

I made sure I told everyone close to me about the last assault. It seemed as if I was making a living will, only this would be evidence in case the worst happened and Sam actually killed me next time. I barely scraped through everyone's total surprise reactions. If they had suspicions, they had mastered the art of concealing them. Then I told Sam that everyone now knew, that he could relax in front of them now and let his true self appear, that he didn't have to appear as Mr Sweetness and Light. He wasn't impressed, but then neither was I. My nerves became overwhelming. I bit my nails at a constant rate, and when they were stunted and ugly, I bit my fingers. The constant pressure on my neck muscles meant headaches and tender shoulders. Sometimes I couldn't rest the strap of my handbag on them. I marvelled at nature's alarm bells, warning me of the danger I was in.

The day of the appointment with the psychiatrist duly arrived, much looked forward to by me. I sat wearily down in front of the doctor and explained everything to him. I detailed all the incidents and punishments over the years, and Sam defended every one. The doctor was an older gentleman, dressed in tweed suit and with glasses which he peered over. He scribbled frantically as I barbled on and on, sometimes crying, sometimes angry, depending on which incident I was describing. I worried that we might be given a repeat pep talk, similar to the one our GP had given, but hoped the we would receive some constructive help. 'Sometimes I think I am wasting my time doing things like this.' I talked to him as if Sam wasn't even there. 'You know, maybe I'm clutching at straws here, and Sam cannot, or will not be changed from this behaviour. Is there a real chance of any of this helping us?' I was desperate for his answer to be positive.

'Yes. Men can change from the most intensive pattern of emotional and physical abuse.' He began talking to Sam. 'There is some kind of emotional problem here, Sam, but of course there is no point in any of us being here today unless *you* want to change. There has been physical violence in this marriage, and *you* must be responsible for that.' Sam nodded, but I felt great. At last, someone who was not pointing the finger at me and reinforcing Sam's idiotic beliefs. He began to explain his theory to Sam, comparing him with of all things, a water tank!

'You feel perhaps like a water tank, full to bursting with past hurts and unresolved arguments. More water drips into the tank, and you feel like you will burst, and moisture starts to leak from the tank's seams. Then, you burst, and the tank loses a lot of water, perhaps not enough. You and the tank feel much better now, since you are not so full. You can even accept a little water intake, until, of course, things start to reach bursting point again.'

'Yeah, yeah, that's it, that's how I feel,' Sam enthused. This theory had been explained by me to Sam before, I was certain. Perhaps not in those exact descriptions (I never thought about

Sam being like a water tank, that's for sure) but it was the definite pattern all the same. But this was a man who should know what he was talking about and Sam obviously respected his opinion, and point of view, I, on the other hand, was just 'the wife' – who knew nothing. I honestly didn't care, as long as this doctor could wheedle his way into Sam's brain and force him to see that there is a better way to live.

On our way home in the car, Sam chattered confidently about the doctor and his amazing theories. I looked at him warily, wondering if his apparent enthusiasm was another ploy to escape another appointment. But he seemed adamant about attending this doctor and he affectionately rested his hand on mine.

> Monday, 1 August 1994
> . . . Sam has been all over me since the doctor's session with us, and I'm trying to fend him off. I've no romantic feelings for him at all – I'm only just getting used to him cuddling me again.
>
> Last night I slept beside him for the first time in ten weeks! He interpreted that as the green light for sex. My patience is paper thin, but I thought I was tactful in putting him off. Typical man.
>
> I'm still making provisions for leaving. I think about it a lot. I have a sense of survival about me, can't quite explain it. If the psycho works, fine, great etc. If not, I'll be prepared won't I?

While aimlessly wandering around the shopping centre one day with Rosie, I decided to go into the Woman's Aid office. I introduced myself as 'Susan from Ladywell' and the lady who answered the door nodded, respecting my wish to remain anonymous. She led me through to one of several rooms and we sat down on two large old-fashioned chairs that had been part of a suite. There was a bed made up and ready for use in one corner and an enormous toy box in another corner. I launched into my situation details, while Rosie dived head first into the toy box. She listened to me and my theory about Sam's therapy sessions with the psychiatrist.

'Although I feel it an achievement that I've managed to get him to see a doctor . . .' At that sentence, Wanda nodded in agreement. '. . . to be honest, I doubt that it'll actually change anything. I'm really here today to see just what you can offer me, if the worst comes to the worst.' I smiled, feeling rather embarrassed about the admission I had not actually said out loud to anyone before.

She assured me that the organisation was only a phone call away, if disaster did strike. I could call anytime, day or night, it didn't matter to them. She advised me to get my name down onto the council housing waiting list, making sure that the postal address was somewhere else, so that interesting little letters didn't fall onto our own doormat for Sam to see. 'That will also show your intention to leave, if indeed you have to in the future. And, if things work out all right, you can then decide whether to accept any offer of a house that comes to you. But do it now, get your name onto the list now, don't wait to see how things go.' She gave me the name of a lawyer whom they had sent other women to, and again she told me to phone him, anytime. I wrote his name in my diary, alongside my friends' addresses. I initialled his first name, as if he was just another acquaintance and I wrote 'Mums & Tots' beside it.

In October 1994, Sam was suddenly suspended from his job as office manager. He was being accused of fiddling his expenses and the week's suspension was to give him time to prove that he hadn't. He professed complete innocence, but was clearly hurt about being accused of such a thing. He immediately presumed that they were looking for a reason to sack him and he told me that he would accept a redundancy package from them, if that was really what they wanted. But Sam had liked his job. He loved the comfort that being one of the longest-serving employees gave him. He recalled sales records had never been broken, and wondered just who they had in mind for his job since he believed he was the only man for it. Moments later he sat weeping gently in his chair.

'Come on, Sam,' I soothed while I hugged him close. 'So they don't want you, it's their loss, the fools. Maybe it's time for change anyway. You have years of experience and ability, this is your chance to get out of a rut. It's a challenge, not a disaster . . .' I sympathised, but rallied him on. I felt sorry for him. I remained optimistic throughout the long week before his final meeting at his office, suggesting firms he could apply to, and businesses he might like to think about running if he did get some kind of redundancy payment. The morning before he was due to leave for Edinburgh saw him subdued, almost resigned to his fate. But my efforts over the past seven days had not gone unnoticed and he held me firm against him, thanking me sincerely for my strength and support. The moment caught my breath.

Less than three hours later he stepped off the Edinburgh bus, the company car now taken from him. He presented himself the picture of misery, with his dismissal letter firmly clutched inside his hand. There was no mention of any redundancy payment, he had been sacked.

Personally, I had no doubts about Sam pilfering something out of his expenses account. 'Everyone does it,' he assured me once before, and he often felt that his firm owed him more than the yearly salary that they paid him. It was a small price to pay for his genius within the sales office, according to the man who was now truly unemployed.

Of course, this also meant that our monthly appointments with the psychiatrist had to be halted. The private health insurance that we enjoyed was part of a long-service entitlement supplied by Sam's former employers. Two sessions were all that we managed and I hoped that even that would help us.

We stopped our moaning and got on with life, such as it was. We immediately went onto Income Support with government help to pay the mortgage on the house. At least we wouldn't be homeless. I applied to go onto a training scheme for qualifications in computer skills. Although my secretarial skills were still fresh, the need for computer knowledge was an absolute must when applying for jobs. Sam applied for anything and everything even remotely suitable, and was even securing the odd interview. There was apparently nothing for him in his trade, and former friends and colleagues made themselves painfully noticeable by their complete avoidance of him.

When a place on my course became available I joined the training scheme which involved full-time learning, This meant that Sam would be 'house husband' at home with the children all day. He took up the role completely and without complaint. The role reversal was thorough and interesting for Mum and me to observe.

On my return from training, or 'work' as we called it, I would come into the hall and Rosie would run to meet me. Sam would be in the kitchen, as I had been only months before, and my tea would be ready, placed on the table, ready to eat. We would recount our day to each other, over noisy children asking him questions rather than me. He dealt completely with Rosie, even during her transition from nappies to the potty. He also took her to the local Mother and Toddlers group, often the only man present. Sam attended a government course looking at ways to set up a new business. After much research we settled on a business venture which we thought would suit us both and hold our interest as well. We quickly set about using the material which Sam had gained during his course, and formatted a business plan. We had nothing behind us except for the house, but I was more than ready to put it up for a guarantee if it meant we would be employed again. Sam soon began making appointments to see the business managers, and interest was non-existent at first. The third bank that he approached, however, asked him for two interviews before tentatively offering us a loan almost at the amount of capital we had estimated. However, when the time came for Sam to sign the various forms that would set the financial ball rolling, he made a sudden announcement.

'I don't think we should do this, Susan. I've changed my mind. I'm worried that the shop will fail, and we'll be homeless. We can't lose the house, we'd be nowhere, going nowhere. It's too much of a risk, I can't do it. I'm sorry.'

23 May 1995
Millionaire status and secure job prospects are once more torn from my grasp. Sam announced that he didn't want to put the house up for collateral for the loan. I was *so* disappointed. Again, I feel him holding me/us back. He decides now to 'play safe' when he was Mr Fucking Arrogance while he was Office Manager and his 'they'd never get rid of ME' attitude. I wasted my time looking forward to it, and encouraging him and convincing him that we could do it. And we could have. He didn't even think we could get this far. There is an interview for a Trade job coming up, and I suspect that this was the reason for his change of heart. Bastard.

So we had to let it all go. If I thought I could set it all up myself, carry on myself, I would have. But it was Sam who had completed the course, and it was he that would receive the government help. He was not prepared to go ahead with it, so we all did without. Although I accepted his decision without fuss, I felt very bitter. I completed my course and gained my certificate in less than five months. For me it was back to the Jobcentre, and general home life and housework. For Sam, it meant continual interviews, with usually no comeback on the result. He had decided though, after his interview with a firm, to attend the same training scheme that I had gone through. Using our unemployed time constructively meant that at least we would be gaining qualifications, every five months or so.

Friday, 2 June 1995

The day of the interview, and Sam comes downstairs and immediately attacked Ryan for some misdemeanour. I couldn't get the full story from Sam, but stood painfully silent while he smacked Ryan hard over his legs for calling his Dad 'an idiot'. Then less than ten minutes later Ryan got up from his chair, still crying, and inadvertently stumbled over Rosie's shoes which were lying on the floor. Sam roared at the boy viciously, telling him to pick them up. His venomous gesturing was manic and I tried to warn him to calm down. Ryan kicked the door open on his way up the stairs. God, you'd think he'd emptied his bowels onto the carpet the way Sam jumped up and raced after Ryan. He charged up the stairs behind Ryan, who was shouting for help from me. Sam lifted him up by his sweater, so that his red angry face was in line with poor Ryan's, and then he threw him onto his bed – from the hall!

I was *furious*. Sam was angry at me for not standing by him throughout this ridiculous persecution. He then reverted to his bad old ways by trying to annoy me, he even had the gall to accuse me of protecting the boy because he was Keith's son! Then he told Rosie not to breathe too loud near her brother, lest I should object. *Bastard*. I am seething with anger, I want to rip his bloody head off! Bloody hard luck if he is annoyed at me protecting Ryan. It's a bloody sin that the boy needs protecting from a supposedly grown man posing as a responsible parent.

I had no idea how the interview had gone. Sam was once more living in his silent world. I thought more about poor Ryan, and ran the entire episode over in my mind all day, trying not to get upset each time. He had landed, thankfully, on David's bed, and fell onto the floor, when Sam had launched him into the air. He was both shaken and shocked. 'He's done that before you know, Mum,' he said, while David nodded silently. 'Sometimes he picks us up by our sweaters and shouts into our faces. I hate it when he does that.' He snarled and punched the settee. 'He just likes to be smart with us. It's like he feels tough or something when he's throwing us around like that,' David added.

'Well, we know that bullies like to pick on people smaller than themselves, that's just what Dad is doing. But I promise you both, he will not be allowed to do anything like that again.' And I meant what I said.

If there was a tie that bound us, it was broken. If there had been any respect left for Sam, then it was gone now, along with any love or affection too.

I climbed the stairs that night, regardless of that morning's events, and I got into our bed. I purposely looked at Sam, who was reading as usual, and asked him how his interview went.

'Fine,' he spat out grudgingly. It was exactly what I wanted to hear. I didn't want him to save himself by suddenly becoming amenable. But this was supposed to be my cue to attempt to cajole him into some kind of conversation. I was supposed to ignore his constant insults and beg him to speak properly to me. But I didn't. He had actually released me from all that, by totally reverting back to his silent ways. I simply rose from the bed for the last time and after picking up my handbag I went downstairs to sleep on the couch.

I filled out the application form for council housing, with strict instructions about the postal address. I posted it off, regretting not having done it sooner, as I had been advised.

Monday, 5 June 1995

Day three – and the silence goes on. So what. You see, I'm no longer going by the script. Before, I would have been trying pathetically to get him to talk, say something. Giving up any remaining dignity I had to have him forgive me my sin. (What sin?) Now, he is a confused little man. I'm not 'coming across' as usual. The little hamster is turning that wheel faster each day. I haven't responded to any of his little signals, which would have been pounced upon by me as the green light for begging. Ryan told he, however, that he did apologise to him for the interview incident. Wow. It doesn't mean that he won't do it again.

By week three we were still barely acknowledging each other's existence. Mum had warned me that what I was doing was just as petty, but she failed to see that I had no heart to continue with the relationship that Sam and I had any more. He would pat his sons lovingly on the head, showing the world what a great guy he was but he tripped himself up one day when he threatened to slap David hard if he didn't stop doing something. I made a point of explaining something to him. It was the first time in three weeks that I had said anything other than 'yes' or 'no' to him.

'From this moment on Sam, you are no longer allowed to physically assault any of these children ever again. That includes lifting them, pushing, pulling, dragging, slapping or smacking them anywhere. If they need disciplining, then you can ground them until I get home and I will deal with it. Other than that, you keep your hands off them. Understand?' He was mad with anger. But I continued to ignore him.

'They'll walk all over you, you stupid cow! They're bloody little hooligans, and they can do what they like now, eh? Not in my house they won't!' he raged. He slammed the door on his way out,

Desperate to stay one step ahead of Sam, I decided to pack a bag for the boys and me, and hid it in the small toilet cupboard. I anticipated him arriving home that evening and ordering the boys out of 'his house'. Inside the bag were clothes for all of us, including for Rosie. He didn't do anything like that, but had decided to ignore David and Ryan completely instead.

It was obvious that he was trying, however late in the day. The following day saw him jovial and casting aside his decision to reject them by talking freely with his sons. On his return from his course, he appeared friendly and talkative, enthusiastically telling me about a factory that had suddenly gone ablaze. He even pushed himself to tell me some details about another job that he was about to apply for, despite my obvious disinterest in what he had to say. I felt slightly embarrassed for him sometimes, and wondered if indeed he had felt the same way when it was me that was trying hard to gain conversation between us. But I was lost to him now. I could hardly look at him. I barely referred to him about anything, preferring to make decisions about the children by myself. I made no small talk, no goodbyes or hellos.

My mind worked overtime, deciding on the best plan that

would make a way out for me and the children. Although the time just wasn't quite right, I knew it would be soon. Every evening we sat watching television, sitting as far apart from each other as possible. I would get up to go to bed and watch the television in the bedroom until he came thumping lethargically upstairs. Then, keeping a promise to myself, I would in turn go back into the living-room to sleep on the couch. There was no need to explain myself or my actions and I felt reasonably calm and at ease.

CHAPTER EIGHT

On the morning that I had made up my mind about the rest of my life I sent David and Ryan to school as usual. Rosie stood at the glass outer door, waving pathetically to them as she did every schoolday. The boys were looking forward to the school holidays, there was only one week to go until the end of term.

Sam was also at the start of a fortnight off from the training centre and had enjoyed a long lie in that morning. I had a mental monologue that had short sentences, blunt and to the point. I wanted Sam to completely understand all that I was about to tell him. He reacted with surprise when I approached him, and I sat down at the kitchen table, hoping he would too. He stood at the window instead, with his fat arms folded over his chest. Unexpectedly, he was smiling and with a certain amount of horror I realised that he was expecting some kind of apology. He thought that I wanted to patch things up between us!

'It's not what you think. But I'd like you to listen to me first before, hopefully, we can both discuss what I am about to say.' I took a breath. 'I would like us to formally separate. I don't think we should carry on any more. I don't want to. I've consulted a lawyer . . .' I lied, '. . . and, if we can agree on a separation date, we can both still stay in this house for the next two years. Things will be pretty much the same as they have been over the past six weeks really.' There was no change of expression, there was no reaction from him. 'If we both apply for housing, I presume that one of us will be offered a house during the two years' separation. And, after two more years, the children will be older, Rosie will be four, it will be easier for her to get used to access times between us. I fully expect to gain custody of the children, presuming that you are more likely to be employed that I am,' I lied again. 'I have no intention of keeping Rosie from you, Sam. I will do everything in my power to make sure you have as much access as you want to all the kids. I'm sorry Sam,' I ended curtly, 'that is what I want.' I don't think I even finished my last word before Sam launched into his own speech. He began issuing his orders, it was the reaction I had expected from him.

'Right. First of all, separated or not, *you* will be the one moving out of this house, not me. You apply for housing, you can move out, taking the boys with you whenever you like. You can take all your belongings, but you will sign over your half of the house to me.'

'Why?'

'Let's just say it's your punishment. If you want out, then you lose your entitlement to the house. I will be applying for custody of Rosie, you will not be allowed to take her with you, the boys can go now for all I care. Separation or divorce, while you stay in this house you will cook and clean for me, or you can pack your bags this minute, or better still . . . ' he added menacingly, 'I'll do it for you.' And with that, he left the kitchen, took his jacket and the building society book and left the house alone.

I spent the entire day thinking hard about the situation, but had no regrets in telling Sam about my intentions. I phoned Mum and told her and she accepted that there would be some kind of backlash from that morning's talks. She assured me that she would be available if help was needed. I presumed that Sam had gone away to think about it. I appreciated the shock behind my cool statements, but I was prepared to ride the inevitable storm. When David and Ryan arrived home, I sat them down also and briefly outlined the situation, telling them that Sam had been away all day, and that I did not know what to expect from him when he returned.

'Do you think he will let us stay here?' David asked hopefully.

'I don't know, son. But Nana knows what's happening, she'll always be there to help us if we can't,' I reassured him. They nodded obediently, and asked to go out to play, taking Rosie with them. I then looked up the name in my diary that I had hoped I would never need.

John Hanrahan latched onto my situation almost immediately and, without expanding too much on my current options, he insisted I go down to his office to talk. We hurriedly made an appointment for the following day.

My thoughts continued to jumble inside my head and I desperately hoped that Sam would see sense and agree to some kind of separation, formal or not. I was sure that he wouldn't want to carry on with our marriage like this, and hoped that he wouldn't see my wanting out as revenge. I waited for his return and watched our children playing happily in the evening sunshine.

At last he appeared, incredibly drunk and clutching a carrier bag full of beer cans. He almost knelt down to deposit his cans into the fridge, and stumbled backwards for a second.

'Are you okay?'

'Fine,' he said, smiling at me, and he turned to go into the living-room where the children now were. Sam had only been this drunk perhaps twice throughout our whole marriage, and his apparent sobriety unnerved me.

'Right, listen up,' he stated to all in front of the television, 'you may no longer call me "Dad", I am not your father, I am only Rosie's father. She is the only one allowed to call me that.' My heart sank on hearing this, and almost immediately both boys came through to the kitchen. They were scared and uptight about Sam's drunken appearance. I made the tactical decision to send them across to Mum's house for the night, reminding them about the packed bag still lying inside the toilet cupboard. They both dived for the door, like rats deserting a doomed ship, and I almost wished I could have gone with them. Ryan stopped in the hall, however, to give me a kiss and a quick cuddle. I held back the beginnings of tears, just waiting to burst into my eyes, and waved them off. 'At least they are out of it,' I told myself. I had to stay behind with him, because of Rosie.

The living-room door was suddenly closed to me, and I was aware of him talking to someone. It was Marjery, and I stood as close to the door as I could to try to listen. 'She's my wee girl . . . no one is taking her away from me . . . a divorce as soon as possible . . . No, there isn't a section out on her yet, but she's to stay with me at all time . . .'

My heart raced into action until I thought I'd be sick, and I tried to stay calm as I waited for him to finish his slurred conversation and sit down again. Feelings of absolute dread covered me, making me numb with shock. I opened the door, and watched him slump down onto the settee, while Rosie climbed clumsily onto his knees, totally unaware of his inebriated state.

'Sam, are you planning on taking Rosie away from me?' I had to know.

'Yes,' he answered almost triumphantly. 'I've been to my lawyer and I'm getting divorced from you. I'm accusing you of being an unfit mother, because that is what you are. Rosie must stay with *me* at all times. Understand?' His breathing was laboured, and his eyelids seemed weighted. He was so drunk he could hardly keep his eyes open, nor hear the innocent chatter of his daughter as she tried to gain his attention. I sat still, on the edge of my chair, without answering him, my mind fighting for answers about what to do next. There were so many things that I wanted to do. I wanted to lift something incredibly heavy and smash it down on him while he sat stupefied and marinating in lager. I wanted to grasp Rosie from him and run for the door, but every time I answered her questions, he would spring to life, clasping her close to him. He could read my mind. I wanted to strangle his fat, cumbersome neck. I hated him.

Suddenly, he jumped up and lifted the baby into his arms. Without a word he took her upstairs and, I presume, put her to bed. My chance had gone, for another night anyway.

I sat trembling, biting my nails for comfort. I was and felt truly alone that evening, not even hearing Mum's voice over the phone helped. I consoled myself with the hope that he would be past his drunken speech about sections, and keeping Rosie close to him all the time, by the morning. I hoped, too, that the hangover he would get would be the worst one in the entire universe.

I hardly slept at all that night. Sam was up and wandering about the house more than once, and even appeared at the door of the living-room as if he was checking on me. Since I couldn't tell in the dark whether he was still drunk or not I remained silent, pretending I was asleep. But, his stumbling about worried me, and I hoped Rosie was still in her own bed. When morning did come, and I had slept for a while, Rosie came downstairs as usual and burst happily into the room. We cuddled each other as she chattered on without a care. Meanwhile, I wondered what the new day would bring. After feeding and dressing Rosie, I prepared myself for the journey into Livingston and my meeting with John Hanrahan. Sam thumped rhythmically downstairs and sat himself gently onto the edge of the couch. He grimaced as Rosie squealed her greeting and roughly began climbing onto his legs. He may have managed to step downstairs without tripping, as I had maliciously hoped, but at least he did have the hangover of the century.

'Are you taking Rosie with you? I take it you are going into town,' he said without raising his head to look at me. I fully expected him to deny me her company. I did want to take her, but tried not to show it.

'If I'm allowed to.'

He waved his hand in a gesture that almost said, 'Did you really believe that line last night?' I scooped her up into my arms before he changed his mind.

During the bus journey into Livingston I tried to put all the jumbled events into some kind of order. I had left Rosie with Mum and the boys, who were all anxious for news.

John introduced himself confidently and showed me through to his shoe-box size office. He was tall and slightly built, and far too young to be a solicitor in my view. He was the man for the job, though, according to the folk at Woman's Aid. And so I put my faith and almost my entire future in his hands.

He explained several legal procedures that were available and the consequences once these actions had been started. He launched into the divorce process, but I found myself mentally brushing that information aside.

'I'm not really thinking too much about the divorce side of things just now, John. I am desperately trying to keep our children together, and more importantly with me, while Sam has designs on going for custody of Rosie. What terrifies me most just now is the thought that he'll just take her away again, and it doesn't need to be that far away for me not to be able to see her again . . .'

'Has he taken her away without your consent before?'

'Yes, last year when she was just a year old, but he brought her back the next day. Apparently he had been at his Mum's with her, but if he decided to take her up to Stirling again tomorrow, he could stay up there permanently. I'd hardly see her . . . we've no transport you see, his Mum would believe his every word . . .' I stopped myself before I completely crumbled in front of the man. I wondered how many women, just like me, had sat in his office prattling on about their situation, blinking back tears and swallowing sobs.

'Your situation is somewhat complicated by the formal separation you've suggested to your husband, but it would be possible for you to gain interim custody. This wouldn't prevent your husband from taking your daughter away, but at least if he did, we could then ask the courts to send some officers after him, to get her back. We could set the wheels in motion for that now, if you wish. I would recommend that you do it now. Remember, his lawyer will be advising him of the same procedure,' he warned. It took me barely one minute to decide to go ahead.

Amidst all this hectic confusion inside my head, at least one priority remained crystal clear to me. Sam was rejecting the boys, quite blatantly too. Whatever information he had already received from his lawyer was obviously centred on Rosie and his wish for custody of her. Lame threat or not, I had to take the lead in all this, or risk splitting up the children.

'Now remember. Your husband will be entitled by law to receive a copy of these court papers, and they could be landing on your doormat by Wednesday.'

'I'll handle it,' I lied, trying to sound confident. 'At least he'll know what my intentions are, and that I'm not bluffing.'

Outside, I felt light-headed with tension. My appetite had all but deserted me, but my body needed fuel. I automatically headed towards the bus station to get back to the kids.

The district was buzzing with children it seemed, enjoying the freedom that warm summer days bring. Rosie was napping, sprawled untidily on her Nana's living-room couch. David and Ryan dived into the house to say quick hellos to me, before being called out to play by other tousle-headed pals. I urged them to go, not wanting them to hear my news. Mum's close friend and neighbour was visiting, and both women were eager to hear what had happened at the lawyer's office.

'Quite right, hen,' they both chorused, and then laughed at the way they had both spoken in perfect unison. We had few secrets from May, and she was an incredibly loyal friend who defended my every action against Sam. She considered him brutish and irresponsible towards the children, and she puffed continuously on several cigarettes during the hour I spent explaining the various legalities that I had learnt. Mum and May, both in their sixties, made excellent company for each other, without abusing their relationship by spending too much time together. They respected each other's need for time alone and with their respective families.

Both women speculated about Sam's next move, once he discovered I was going for interim custody.

'He'll give up. He'll step back in shock once he realises you mean business,' Mum said.

'I know this sounds pessimistic but personally I think Sam will fight me every step of the way. Everything I do now will be just another reason for revenge. He'll go for full custody of Rosie even if he really doesn't want it. Just so long as I don't get her.'

'What do you think he'll do when he sees the court papers?' May asked.

'I don't really want to think about it. I've still got to get through today, and tonight,' I sighed wearily.

I arranged to leave the boys at their Nana's for another night and began walking home with Rosie. I said nothing to Sam. As far as he knew, I had spent all day at the centre. Once Rosie was fed, Sam seemed to take charge of her and put her into her pyjamas and into her bed.

'So,' I ventured, 'what happens next? When does your custody action begin, and when will I be told about it?'

'We are doing nothing until we see what your next move is,' he answered sternly. His eyes never left the television screen. I felt smug about the day's decision I had made at my lawyers. 'You'll soon see what happens next, you sad bastard,' I thought. How typical of him to force me to make the first move. He often left important decisions for me to make during our marriage. That way, if things didn't work out, guess who was to blame? As the weekend drew near, things quietened down slightly. Sam kept himself silent and busy pottering about the house and garden. I brought the boys back to the house to play with their sister, and they told me they felt safe enough to sleep in their own bedroom once more.

Sam blatantly ignored David and Ryan. He would tickle and play with Rosie, but if David attempted to join in, Sam would simply get up to walk away on the pretence of putting her on her swing or to take her out for a walk. I pointedly warned them against approaching Sam, something I had never done before, but encouraged them to continue to play with Rosie. Often I would see Sam sitting out on the patio, watching the children playing together. I could feel him waiting for one of the boys to slip up, to snatch a toy from Rosie's grasp, or to cause her to cry during one of their rough and tumble sessions. I found it hard to concentrate on anything. My suspicions were confirmed when I heard Sam telling Ryan to 'Fuck off' when the child had startled him at some point. At moments like that, I found my suppressed anger almost overwhelming.

The following morning, Sam loudly told Rosie (not me) that they were going out for the day. I immediately challenged him, my heart already thumping loudly inside my chest. 'Where are you going then?'

There was no answer. He smiled, ever so slightly, just enough for me to notice. 'If you are intending to take Rosie away from us, Sam, at least tell me, so that we can say a proper goodbye to her.' Still no answer. His smug silence just shouted out the fact that he could see my utter anguish. I bent down to kiss her hair as she waited excitedly for Daddy to pick her up. I put on her light jacket and kissed her face before he roughly pulled her from me.

I berated myself for appearing so bloody anxious about his 'day out', but I followed them to the door anyway.

'Don't wait up for us,' he said, before closing the door gently.

I wanted to run after them, to be able to find the strength to pull her from his strong arms and run away, anywhere. But I merely stood glued to the floor, watching their images blur behind floods of frustrated tears.

John advised me that there was little that I could do. If he had defected to Stirlingshire, it would be at least a fortnight before the interim custody would come into effect. All I could do was wait. 'Christ, he could be anywhere by now. He has all our money,' I told Mum, 'he could have hired a car and be halfway to London for all I know.' Poor Mum arranged to come for a visit to the house immediately, and I felt guilty about all the time I was draining from her. She was my only confidante though, the only person who could advise and encourage me, She would put things into perspective, bringing me down from high hysteria the way my other friends could not.

The day dragged and after Mum had left and I had made the dinner for the boys, we sat peacefully in the kitchen together. I couldn't eat, but nervously tapped my fingers on the side of my coffee cup.

'He'll bring her back, Mum,' Ryan soothed, placing his hand on my back.

'I'm sure he will pet,' I forced a smile. 'Look boys, I'm sorry about all this. Things must be really hard for you both, but you know I'll do everything I can to keep Rosie with us, don't you?' They nodded.

'It's not your fault . . . it's that fat git's. Remember, it's him that should be saying sorry!' David pointed his finger towards the window, and the general outside. 'S'pose he's not going to be our Dad now,' he added.

'Of course he's not,' Ryan shot back, 'he doesn't love us any more.'

'Did you love him?'

'Used to . . . but not any more,' Ryan said, but David preferred not to answer my question and I didn't press for one. I decided to explain things to them later, when the situation didn't seem so raw and tender.

At 9.45 p.m. that evening, Sam arrived back at the house with Rosie, who looked wide eyed, and excited. I opened my arms to pick her up, so relieved to see her, but Sam beat me to her and smartly carried her straight upstairs. I heard her chattering loudly to him as I envisaged him putting her to bed. I dearly wished that I could have at least felt her warm little body against mine while I hugged her close, But I showed little emotion when he had snatched her up from me, and felt glad that she was at least sleeping in her own bed that night. Quietly I phoned Mum, to tell her that they had returned safely, before spreading my sleeping bag over the settee and climbing into it.

Saturday came and went, a glorious day that saw the children playing outside nearly all day. Sam restricted himself to the patio, and he sat with cans of lager, reading a book and talking to Rosie. I busied myself with the housework, but preferred not to leave the house in case Sam refused to let me take Rosie out too. I wasn't looking for any kind of confrontation. On the Sunday morning, after a relatively peaceful night, I ventured out to Mum's house for a welcome break from the tense atmosphere that lay thick and sour around Sam and me. I stayed only a short while though. The thought that Sam might take Rosie away, grasping his opportunity with glee, stayed with me. I had asked the boys only to come to see Mum. I wanted Sam to think that I trusted him enough to leave my daughter in his care. They were still there when we did return.

That afternoon though, Mum phoned me. 'I didn't want to tell you this in front of the boys, Susan, but the wee fella let it slip that they both go to their beds fully dressed. When I asked them why, Ryan said that they had decided to do this in case Sam attacked you during the night. Apparently, they've got tennis rackets beside them. They've worked out a plan where David runs to a next door neighbour, and Ryan batters Sam, to stop him hitting you.'

'Oh Jesus . . .'

'Is he listening?'

'Yeah.'

'Right, well, I think they should come here tonight. Poor wee lambs can't even sleep sound in their own beds at night for fear of that bastard.'

'Of course, that's great.' I kept my answers short and sweet, while Sam gazed at me, listening intently.

'So send them around, after tea. And, take care. We'll keep in touch.'

While I was preparing the tea, I became aware of shouts and screams coming from the living-room. It was Sam, and his roaring seemed to rattle the house. He was shouting at someone, one of the boys. Ryan ran into the kitchen, closely followed by Sam.

'I didn't do anything Mum . . .' Ryan stammered, his face ashen with shock.

'Aye you did!' Sam screamed at the boy. He was covered in sweat it seemed, his twisted face was gleaming with it. 'He kicked Rosie's toy across the living-room, he did it deliberately!' He lowered his head towards Ryan, who was almost cowering under the table with fear. Sam reached forward, pulling him into a standing position, and I gripped the closest kitchen utensil I could find, which turned out to be a fish slice.

'I never, I never did,' Ryan yelled back at him bravely.

'Lying little cunt that you are, do you think you're safe because you run through to Mummy every time you try something on . . .'

'Calm down, Sam.'

'You need a bloody good doing, and that's what you'll fuckin' well be gettin' if you touch any of her toys again!'

'Calm down, Sam.'

'*All* of this, *all* of this is *your* fault,' he continued, pointing at Ryan. 'And you!' he shouted at me, 'you get yourself and your bastards out of this house, or I'll do it for you!' The sweat was now dripping from his chin, landing in circles on the floor at our feet.

'Oh yeah? And how are you going to do that, eh?' I pointed the fish slice menacingly close to his fat, crimson face. I wished that it had been a sizeable breadknife. But he eyed it suspiciously, stepping back from Ryan before adding arrogantly, 'Oh, I'll think of something.'

We hadn't stopped shaking by the time we were sitting around the table trying to eat. Rosie squealed and chattered constantly beside us, while Sam sat in the living-room. Both lads were pale and sullen. When I told them that they could go to their Nana's that night, they visibly cheered up. I ached for the strain that was so obviously upon their little shoulders. I didn't actually want them to go, but I knew it just wasn't safe here. They were no longer safe in their own home.

David and Ryan left for the walk to their Nana's house. They took nothing with them, and they actually ran once they had waved goodbye to me. I blew kisses, trying to smile, trying to show them that things weren't that bad. But they were,

I chased Rosie upstairs, and she giggled and screeched with excitement. She loved her bathtime, and she began peeling off clothes before she had reached the top of the stairs. I tried hard to concentrate on what I was doing with her. I wanted to sit down and cry. I wanted to scream out loud, to release the incredible tension that weighed me down. My stomach burned because there was nothing in it. My head ached with the strain that I felt. I made up mental sentences that forced me to go on. 'Carry on, you can do this. Carry on, you can do this,' I repeated them over and over, while I played with my daughter in her bath.

On a trip to her bedroom for some pyjamas I heard him talking on the phone again. I tip-toed downstairs, flinching at the creaky stair boards making their noise.

'Yeah . . . I'll be there about 11 in the morning, so expect us about then . . .'

He was taking her away again. My heart quickened its beat, working overtime with the state of fright my body was in. Another day without her, another night waiting for him to bring her home. I tried to dry Rosie and dress her for bed as if nothing had happened. I ached to ask him if he was taking her back up to his Mum's, even composing a light-hearted sounding sentence in my head. But, I couldn't see much point. I didn't trust him, even if he did answer me this time. We sat in silence, watching television. I imagined this night to be our last together, with Rosie becoming drowsy and wriggling on my knee.

Eventually, he stood up and reached down to pick up our daughter. She sat limply on his arm as he brushed past me and climbed the stairs. I listened for the normal noises, realising that it had been ages since I had actually put her to bed myself. I hadn't kissed her goodnight for days now. After a while I realised that Sam was still moving around upstairs and I stood at the living-room door which was slightly ajar.

I could hear our wardrobe doors being pushed backwards and forwards, but not rhythmically. Drawers were being opened, I could recognise the sounds after years of constant use. He was packing. He was taking her away for good this time. I sat down, fidgeting and forcing my nails into my mouth, to be bitten further and further down the quick. I tried to create options that were open to me now, solutions to this new problem. I trawled my brain for answers to questions about what I could do to stop him.

I flinched when the phone rang and jumped up to answer it. 'Mum,' I felt relief at hearing her voice.

'I think he's packing this time, I can hear him moving about, he's packing some clothes. Mum, I'm so frightened he's taking her away for good this time,' I explained tearfully.

'Jesus, I've a good mind to come up there and kick the cowardly bastard all the way to Stirling myself! The boys told me what happened at teatime, the bullying little prick . . . are you sure you think he's packing?'

'Yeah. It's another fortnight before the custody thing will work for me, and he was only up at his Mum's the day before yesterday. I don't know what to do.' I cried pathetically.

'Look, sit tight for now pet. Do you want me to come up? I could get May to sit with the boys.'

'No, it's okay, it would only unnerve them.'

'Right, keep listening, and if he comes downstairs, ask him. It's worth a try. I'll phone back about every hour. Take care.' And she was gone. I felt sick. I clutched my stomach and wandered around the room, while I scraped up the nerve to climb the stairs

and ask him what his plans were. He was lying on top of our bed.
The television was blaring and he turned to look at me.

'Are you going up to Stirling with Rosie tomorrow?'

'No,' he said quietly. I returned to the stairs immediately. I
couldn't have asked him any more, since I needed time to process
what he had just said. I went over his conversation with the
somebody on the phone. Especially the part when he said 'expect
us at 11'. So if it wasn't his Mum he was talking too, where the
hell was he taking her?

I wandered aimlessly about the living-room, feeling
desperately alone but with a crowded mind. When the phone
rang I sprang over to it.

'I phoned your brother, Malcolm,' Mum began as if
continuing a train of thought, 'to see if he could come over, but
he's got friends round and they're drinking – he can't drive. But
he did say that you should just go to a refuge . . .'

She fell silent while I thought about the suggestion.

'I think I have to be assaulted before they'll take me in though.
Sam hasn't hit me for over a year now.'

'Well,' she brightened, 'I'll give them a phone, see what they
say, eh?'

The phone rang so quickly it seemed obvious that the
emergency phone lines were closed or something. 'They said not
to wait until he hits you,' Mum stated officiously. 'They said you
should get yourself out now.' Then her tone changed to one of
encouragement. 'You could get Rosie out. Just wait till he's
snoring and lift her.'

'No, I couldn't,' I whined. 'I'm too frightened. He'd kill me,
he'll be listening for something . . . I could never run away
carrying Rosie on my hip, she's too heavy for me now.' Dark
visions of stumbling down the stairs with Rosie in my arms
cancelled out the suggestion immediately.

'Well, get up first thing and take her down to the shop for
some milk. Throw your milk away . . .' she added.

'No. I never do that. It would be too suspicious . . . look, I'll
think of something.' She'd helped me make up my mind. 'I'll get
out and I'll go to a refuge. Anything is better than this.'

'They said anytime and anywhere mind, they'll just send a
taxi.'

'I'll think up something,' my voice began to break. 'You'll have

92

to take me when you see me, it could be during the night mind.'

'Don't worry about that, I'll be ready.'

I sobbed into the mouthpiece quietly, my knees almost buckling with the weight of my problems pressing upon me.

'Okay pet,' Mum said quietly, 'I'll see you whenever . . . take care . . . see you soon.'

CHAPTER NINE

'Carry on, you can do this. Carry on, you can do this.' That beautiful summer's day was ending. Brightly coloured Livingstone daisies had already closed their petals in the rockery part of the garden, sleeping peacefully in their little clusters, as I had planted them only weeks before. 'Be strong, get stronger. Be strong, get stronger,' I repeated to myself.

I felt relieved that I'd have somewhere other than Mum's to run to. Surely the woman that Mum spoke to would be true to her word. They would get a taxi when I called them. They'd be on the ball in situations like this, I convinced my worried thoughts.

Mentally, I fixed my sights onto the best possible result for me that night, and worked my way back from that. I had to get Rosie away from the house and Sam as quickly and cleanly as possible. Preferably without damage to either one of us, so it couldn't be a reckless escape. It had to be planned.

Whether Sam had suspicions about my trying to leave with Rosie or not I did not know but I had to assume that he did. I ran over my options for escape in methodical fashion.

I could call a taxi myself, keep the door open and brazenly run upstairs, grabbing Rosie and hurtling back down and outside to freedom. The idea was dangerous if feasible, but the fact that I had no money to pay for the taxi was an added problem.

However, lifting Rosie before I called a cab, or after it arrived, made for more complications when what I needed was a simplistic approach. Furthermore, the outside door was not only locked, but the keys, Sam's keys, weren't in the lock. I searched about my bag for my own, but looking for them in the dark seemed a hopeless task while the initial idea was sinking fast as a possibility.

The year before Sam had bought himself a brand new mountain bike. His intention, he'd explained, was to cycle around the paths of Livingston for exercise, and he announced that he could take the boys on their bikes for picnics. He did that however only once. Since then the bike had remained untouched until I asked to buy a baby carrier for Rosie. She loved her bike seat and although it was a man's cycle and far too big for me, I gained my balance quickly enough with Rosie firmly belted into her seat behind me. It was a cheap form of transport for me and proved great entertainment for Rosie. It was stored along with the boys' bikes in the garage, no doubt behind them, amongst a tangle of brake wires and chains. But time was on my side for once and I reckoned I could spend time slowly freeing it. But getting it outside posed a problem, even if I did have the patience to find my own house keys to open the door. Could I manoeuvre it quickly through the vestibule and down the high steps at our door with Rosie seated in her chair? Forget that one.

My mind began to wander while I gazed into a black and grey garden waiting for inspiration. Is this what Linda did, that night some six years before? Had she been any more organised when Sam had gone to the pub for his pint, presenting her with the opportunity to go? Had she been just as scared? Had she looked around their home that night, at the walls she'd papered and the floor she'd hoovered maybe for the last time, like I did?

It had only taken her two years to get to that final decision to leave him – it had taken me five. She was 18 and just a child, but she knew when to get out. She hadn't dragged any dependants through seriously deep shit in her quest to find true love and happiness – like I had. She didn't have a previous relationship to hear about, that screamed out warning after warning to her – like I had.

'Be strong, get stronger. Be strong, get stronger.'

By 2 a.m. I was close to making up my mind. I made one last visit to the toilet and could hear Sam's rhythmic snoring filtering down from our bedroom. There were two doors to open before getting to the garage, and I jammed their hinges with tea-towels so that they wouldn't close on me.

I peered into the coolness of the garage, searching for the bikes. I stepped into the darkness, determined not to reach out for the switch, mindful of the fluorescent light's distinctive hum that seemed to vibrate throughout the house when it was on.

Sam's bike was indeed hemmed in by David's racer and Ryan's muddy BMX. I set about moving them slowly, quietly, my limbs sometimes trembling with the strain of the procedure, until the bike was free and I pushed it towards the large outer door. I squinted hopefully at the door's handle trying to see if it was locked or not. This was the only serious doubt in my plan, that the garage door would not open. Its hinges screeched and squealed distinctively when the door was ever moved, and I glanced around the shelves hoping that there would be a handy can of oil within my reach. There wasn't, so I checked the bike once more, moving Rosie's seat belts back ready for her when the time came.

I lingered on the step at the connecting door, straining my eyes in the gloom, checking that my intended path to the bike was clear and that it was as far away from any entanglement as possible. I mentally rehearsed my plan once more, and with a final glance at the door I decided to take a fatalistic view to it opening for me.

Of all of my children, David and Rosie were the two that always woke up with the birds. Regardless of our efforts to encourage them to sleep longer as toddlers, they still woke up at 5 a.m. every day. David, now ten, could lie in until perhaps 6 a.m., sometimes 7 a.m. if we were lucky. Rosie still opened her eyes feeling fully refreshed and ready for action at the same godless hour. My plan relied on this habit of hers, and the knowledge that Sam was too damned lazy to get up with her that early. Knowing that I was downstairs, he'd send Rosie down to Mummy. Only this morning would be like no other.

I stretched out on the settee, still dressed, and arranged the sleeping bag over me. I instructed my brain to wake me before Rosie did. I had blatantly used my body like a machine over the past weeks, forcing it to operate, to carry on under such stress and without food or rest. I had no doubts that my brain would also obediently comply.

At 5.05 a.m. I woke with a start. Rosie was up, and I could hear her thumping about upstairs – she was heading for Sam's room. I jumped up and immediately started to gather the essentials I could now see in the light.

Rosie's shoes, an odd cardigan, five nappies, one of Ryan's toy figures, my favourite cup complete with coffee dregs, all stuffed haphazardly into David's schoolbag. My child benefit book, and some milk tokens were tucked down the sides of my handbag before I scanned the bookcase for any more valuables. My mouth felt dry, reminding me of our toothbrushes, but I dismissed the idea, mentally berating myself for not being realistic.

Rosie began to bump her way downstairs, and I hastily slung both bags over my head, and positioned them around my back. My body tingled with anticipation, adrenalin racing through every part of me. I looked back at the connecting door, still open with the tea-towels in place. Thump, thump, thump. She was talking to herself, chattering innocently.

Another quick look at the bookcase and I spotted the house keys, Sam's keys that he had locked the door with before taking Rosie upstairs. I pushed them back under some papers, hoping that his first reaction would be to scrabble for them to open the front door. It would give me even more time, I assured myself.

Finally, she had reached the bottom of the stairs, silently pushing the living-room door open. For a second we looked at each other, transfixed. Me, fully dressed, standing in the middle of the floor laden with bulging bags and smiling weakly. She, a vision in blue Ghostbuster pyjamas, her hair a mess, every strand pointing in a different direction, her cheeks apple red.

I dived towards her, lifting her up before gently closing the door. We walked quickly through to the garage, and without a word between us I sat her in her chair and snapped up her belts.

'Galage, galage, Mummy, we're in the galage!' she twittered excitedly. I jogged back to the connecting door, certain that Sam would have heard her talking. His bedroom was situated directly over the garage. I pulled the towel away from it's hinges and attempted to lock the door behind me. The key refused to turn, merely knocking against the lock's metal insides. The door not being locked meant that Sam could enter the garage after us. I left it, returning to Rosie sitting at a slant while the bike leant against some wooden pallets. 'Goin' a bike, Mummy?' she suddenly asked.

Upstairs, I heard a thump, but concentrated my gaze on the door handle as I bent down to clasp it firmly. I clenched my teeth before forcing it round – and it opened, no problem. Glorious, welcoming sunshine flooded into the garage as the door screeched to its widest limit. The extreme light made us both squint and I instantly felt cheered by its brightness. I mounted the bike while Rosie gleefully stamped her bare little feet inside the footwells, and with one push of the pedal we streaked down the ramp and onto the pavement. I never looked back.

I steered onto the road, the traffic was non-existent. The district was deserted and serene. Rosie chattered about the trees, and the magpies that danced in them, and I answered her as I normally would. I pedalled as fast as was safe for us, and within minutes I was slowing down to enter Mum's estate. The brakes squealed as I stopped outside the cottage, and I could see her jumping up from her chair at the window. She came out, fully dressed and smiling at us both. 'Well done, well done, you're so brave,' she said and sidestepped me to go straight to May's door.

'Look Nana, I'm in my jammies!' Rosie shouted.

'In here with the bike, I'll get the boys,' Mum said, while May gestured to me wildly. 'I have the refuge number,' she rasped as we squeezed into her hallway, complete with Rosie still in her chair. On her table beside the phone was a scrap of paper with two numbers on it. May lifted the baby from her chair and led her through to the kitchen promising biscuits and bananas for her breakfast.

'Hello, yes, well it's me, Susan from Ladywell,' I had no idea who I was talking to. 'My mum phoned you last night . . .' I waited for recognition.

'Oh, aye,' the woman on the other end coughed loudly. 'Aye, yes, I remember,' she gasped, still needing to cough. It was only 5.20 a.m. at this point, but I was desperate for her to control her coughing fit.

'Well, I got away, I'm at this address, can you come to get me?'

'Yes, that's no problem. Get yourself together with the kids, and I will send a taxi,' she sounded more with it now, 'get into the taxi as fast as you can, and stop for no one. Okay?'

The boys appeared, Mum having closed May's door behind them and going back into her own house. David was completely dazed, still rubbing his eyes, while Ryan asked me questions as soon as he saw me. 'What happened, where's Rosie?'

'She's in the kitchen, we got away, and we're getting a taxi somewhere else,' I answered firmly, but I smiled as well, just glad to see them again.

May came through to the living-room, now crowded with bodies, standing expectantly, waiting in silence. She sat on an arm of a chair and puffed a cigarette thoughtfully. 'Well, this is one birthday I will never forget,' she said. We all chorused the same words, and I apologised for her rude awakening.

The knock on the door saw us moving almost in a complete block towards the hallway. May opened the door, glancing outside to make sure that it was Mum, and the taxi had arrived. I imagined Sam's red angry face, screwed up and fierce, and possibly heading our way, but May blocked our progress at the front door. She lightly trotted out and around the pathway to see if anyone was coming, obviously thinking of Sam. Then she signalled her okay and we darted out of the cottage and ran towards the car which was waiting with all its doors open. Rosie bumped heavily onto my hip, but enjoyed the ride all the same. I gave Mum a tearful kiss goodbye as she waited to close my door. I didn't know when I would see her again, or even where we were heading. The driver said nothing and pulled away smartly.

CHAPTER TEN

At the refuge, Isla waited for us all to enter the kitchen before locking the door behind us. After picking us up, the taxi had stopped outside her house and when she'd squeezed herself inside the car she'd turned to introduce herself cheerily.

All seemed silent until another door creaked open enough for someone's face to snatch a quick look at us before disappearing.

'It's all right,' Isla called quietly, and the door opened fully. 'Chris'ake, bloody fright ah got,' a small woman whispered as she pulled her dressing-gown tightly to her chest. Isla motioned us to follow, and we all trooped through to the living-room. The house was spacious with up-to-date furniture and was plainly decorated. Two enormous, new-looking settees dominated the living-room, with the focus being drawn towards the open fireplace, dusted and set, ready to be lit.

Rosie slipped off my knee to pad around the room quietly, while the boys sat sullenly together on one of the settees. We sipped coffee that the small woman had made and Isla hastily introduced her as Debbie from Dundee.

'Heard the latest?' Debbie suddenly brightened, 'he's going to kill himself,' she attempted to smile whilst lighting a cigarette. 'Oh aye,' Isla replied resignedly.

Debbie's voluminous dark, permed hair fell forward, making her face look even smaller and she included me into the conversation. 'This is my man, stayed wi' him for 15 years,' she explained. I nodded, making a quick guess at her age since her slight frame and clear skin made me think she was in her mid 20s. – 'Aye, they'll do anything to get you back in the end. So, Susan,' Isla turned towards me, 'what's your story?'

Not wanting to think about the past nightmarish 24 hours I brushed over the details, trying not to burst into tears after every sentence. The boys listened intently, and when I described my escape on Sam's mountain bike, the women giggled behind their hands in a failed attempt at respecting the seriousness of my story. 'So he's probably still lying in his bed thinking you're downstairs wi' the wean?' they wheezed, coughing between puffs of cigarette smoke. I looked at the boys, before allowing myself to laugh too.

The kids were presented with plates of Weetabix for breakfast, and Isla detailed the rules of the refuge along with what was expected from me in return. 'You can stay here for as long as you wish – you can leave when you like. This is your home, and you are responsible for keeping it clean, safe and tidy for your children, and the other people who live here too. You all have daily chores, on a rota basis, like the dishes, and hoovering etc., and we all expect them to be done. There are no visitors allowed here, no members of your family and *no men!*' Debbie nodded her approval to the last statement. 'There is a pay phone, you can call anyone from there, but don't give out the phone number. No incoming calls, except from your lawyer or us.'

I nodded, expecting more, but Isla finished her coffee and told us she'd take us upstairs to see our room.

'There are two other families in this house, as well as Debbie's', she whispered, and I immediately forgot the names she counted on her fingers. They were all asleep, and I'd meet them later she added. The first landing revealed a row of doors, with only one standing open and that was the bathroom. Isla bumped one door with her hip, and it obligingly popped open. I'd prepared myself for the worst. Black and white images of *Cathy Come Home* documentaries flashed through my mind.

At the worst I'd expected two or three mattresses on a partly carpeted floor, but our room was nothing like that. It boasted two windows and was bright and spacious. It had three beds, neatly made, complete with matching duvets and pillows.

Ill-fitting curtains framed the windows with cream nets, which had originally been white, and the carpet was clean and new. Rosie peeped inside an open drawer in one of two units.

'Oh – it's nice!' I mumbled to the children as we stood in the room's centre.

101

'Yes, it is,' Isla confirmed, looking out onto the farmland view from the main window. 'And it's your room, Susan, try to keep it clean. I hope you'll like it here,' she added, smiling at the boys and smoothing David's hair. 'The folk here just now are nice enough,' she assured me as she stood at the door. The boys sat lethargically on one of the beds, while Rosie thumped across the carpet to climb up on a window seat. 'And if you need to talk, and not to one of the women here, but to one of us, we'll come by for visits during the week. Or feel free to call us at any time, and come up to the office for a cup of tea and a chat,' she smiled.

Sam phoned Mum that night around 9 p.m.

'Can I speak to Susan?' he'd asked calmly.

'She's not here, Sam.' After a short silence, he'd repeated the question.

'She's not here. I don't know where she is.'

'Can I speak to Susan?' His voice was clipped and controlled, and Mum replied likewise.

'She's at a refuge somewhere in Scotland.'

There was silence for a while before he asked in a surprised tone, 'Why?'

'Oh, I don't know,' she said, sounding puzzled, 'could be to do with the fact that her sons are too scared to sleep in their own beds at night, or because her loving husband keeps taking her daughter away for mystery daytrips around Scotland, or maybe she just couldn't stay in the same house as her psychopathic bloody husband any more! What's your theory, eh?' she roared into the mouthpiece. But she couldn't wait for his answer and slammed the phone down instead.

By 11 a.m. Debbie's children had emerged from their bedroom and were assembled in a quiet group in the living-room. Her family consisted of Damen who was 13, Billy ten and their sister Tracey, eight. Billy and Tracey seemed to welcome the boys' arrival at the refuge, and appeared open and friendly towards them. After Isla had left, Debbie and I sat nursing warm cups, while she smoked and I gazed blankly at the television – my thoughts overlapping each other.

Two little girls suddenly ran into the living-room at breakneck speed. The two-year-old was trying to grasp something from her older sister and screeched and complained loudly as the other roared 'No!' at the top of her voice. Debbie and Damen tutted loudly at the noise, raising their eyes to the ceiling and shaking their heads. They screamed some more, and then the older one, aged about four, scurried back towards the hall still fighting off her little sister, whose tear-streaked face was now red with frustration. Rosie struggled onto my knee, gazing in wonderment at the girls.

Their names, as I found out from Debbie, were Jade and Jamie, and their mother, Sonia, padded through from the hall a while later. Ignoring her children, who were still flailing about, she smiled briefly at me as Debbie introduced us, before lighting a cigarette Debbie had offered her and drawing on it with some satisfaction. In contrast to Debbie's smallness, this woman was tall and heavy set, but with a pretty face topped with short, bright red hair. She glanced back at her children, now scrapping fiercely on the carpet behind her, and took a deep breath. 'Fuckin' stop it!' she yelled at them. Jamie broke free from the fight, sobbing pitifully and approached her mother for a cuddle. Sonia lazily draped an arm around the child while she continued a conversation with Debbie who sat curled in the only single chair in the room. Totally engrossed in their subject, they made no attempt to talk to me or to include me in their conversation.

Amongst the noise of the television and the children, my head swam with the enormity of what had happened. Only six hours before I was preparing to leave my own home, and sitting motionless in an unfamiliar room with all these people seemed unreal and dreamlike. I signalled to the boys to come upstairs and they jumped up to follow me, Ryan taking Rosie's hand before one last glance at the girls, now distracted by the cartoons on the television.

I needed money and told the boys that we'd have to travel to the nearest benefits office to sort out an income. 'No, let's stay here,' David pleaded, 'what if Sam sees us?' Two sets of steel blue eyes looked up at me, and I pulled the boys into a quick hug trying to comfort them. 'It'll be okay, we'll just dive out, get some shopping, go to the benefits office and come back. He won't be there, he probably doesn't even know we've left!' I enthused, smiling weakly at them.

Rosie jumped up and down energetically once she knew we

were going out, and I popped my head round the living-room door and Debbie lifted her head from the conversation. 'I'm going out, is there a buggy I could borrow?' I shouted.

'Aye,' she jumped up from her chair, stepping over two children who were stretched out in front of the television, and I followed her through to yet another downstairs bedroom.

Inside, bulging black bags were stacked beside cardboard boxes full of shoes and more clothes. High chairs, obviously second-hand, and baby walkers littered the floor. Two single beds stood unmade beside a cot, the mattress of which was scattered with various toys. Debbie struggled to untangle a buggy from behind a wardrobe. 'There's clothes in here, you can rake around later for stuff for the weans an' that. And don't worry, there'll always be someone here, Jean's not up yet, she'll be in when you get back.'

We walked into town, finding ourselves beside a busy main road. The sky was clear, the day already warm and Rosie settled into her new buggy immediately, while the boys walked beside me.

'Did you see those girls?' they exclaimed in unison.

'Tracey says they're like that all the time!' David said.

'I'm not letting them near Rosie,' stated Ryan defensively, 'they're nutters!'

Tuesday, 11 July
The benefits agency was unreal! Thinking I'd be prepared, I bought rolls and juice for our lunches, comics for the boys and imagined myself fighting with faceless civil servants for a sniff at a tenner.

Instead, I presented myself at the reception area, and after waiting say five minutes to see a clerical officer I launched into my situation details while she tapped away efficiently on her keyboard. Less than 30 minutes later we were cheerily being waved out of the building with all my benefits details having been changed, including my new address at the refuge. I even knew when my next date for payment would be!

John didn't sound surprised that I was calling him from a refuge. We discussed the possibility of Sam moving out of our home, and me moving in, but he doubted we would be successful in court since there were no police reports of previous violence to back up my claims.

I had 101 questions for John, but kept getting side-tracked, and he reminded me that Sam would be receiving the Interim Custody papers today. Good. Hope he cries when he reads them.

I phoned Mum. She sounded tired and relieved to hear me, and I instantly wished we were with her.

She told me that Sam had called her late Monday night, and his apparent surprise at me being at a refuge. We arranged to meet this afternoon, and the boys are visibly cheered at the prospect. Last night, after Rosie had fallen asleep, I sat up to talk with them. They say they're glad we got away but they miss the house, their toys and of course their Nana . . .

We returned from meeting Mum, feeling low and emotional. The hour or so that we had spent in a hastily sought café had gone all too soon, and Mum and I were both tearful on saying goodbye. She stood watching us getting into the taxi that would take us back to the refuge.

Another woman stood in the kitchen and she introduced herself as Jean. She had short mousey brown hair and looked smart in a cropped denim jacket and jeans. Later, once the boys had gone to play with Billy and Tracey and Rosie was napping in our room, I managed to talk with Jean and found her to be the most approachable of the women in the refuge.

She had lived for many years with her violent husband and although she had two children with him, a boy and a girl, only the boy lived with her at the refuge.

She chain smoked her way through her brief history, while folding damp clothes from the washing machine and stacking them neatly on the bunker. She'd endured extreme violence from day one of the relationship. He held down a well-paid job and to outsiders he appeared to be an ordinary, nice guy. Financially they had wanted for little and Jean had presumed that this was her lot in life and that he'd perhaps grow out of it. Jean had run away from him three or four times, but he'd always managed to find her and drag them home. Towards the end, their teenage children Claire and Donald would stand at the door of their home and refuse to stay in if they knew their dad was there before them. They'd merely throw in their schoolbags, electing to stay out of the house for as long as was possible. She spoke with a clear Edinburgh accent, and despite Jean being the sole tenant of their council house in Musselburgh, he'd changed the locks and hidden all her clothes when she'd finally escaped to this refuge.

'Should've done it years ago,' she admitted. 'I remember that morning when he'd gone to work, his face like thunder, and when the bairns came home from school they were telling me: "Come on Mum, let's go now, before he gets back, please, Mum."' She drifted into silent thoughts before brightening slightly. 'He found me again though.'

'What, here?' I was engrossed by her story.

'Aye. He kidnapped Claire, forced her into the car, and drove her back to Musselburgh. Nothing I could do about it,' she said, shrugging her shoulders.

'That's how she stays with him during the week and she comes here at weekends. I miss her, but he just won't leave us alone otherwise. Of course she's 14 now, and says she's happy enough with him, but I don't know.'

Later she told me about the kitchen, and pointed out my cupboard. The cooking arrangements were sometimes done on rota since there were ten children in the refuge, and the sugar, tea and coffee were bought by everyone, for everyone to drink. She pointed out the nearest shop that would accept milk tokens and advised me to use the washing machine as soon as I discovered it was empty since demand was obviously high. 'So, how long have you stayed here, Jean?' I asked, glancing into my somewhat bare cupboard looking for that night's evening meal.

'Eighteen months,' she stated without emotion.

'*What*?' My mind reeled with thoughts of my having to endure such a long stay.

'Oh, aye. You see, we're classed as homeless, but we're not because we actually do have a roof over our heads. So, the points system is crap as far as we're concerned.' Circles of blue grey smoke hung around her, and she blew into the air to disperse them. 'You'll probably get about 160 points, 165 if you're lucky, and that gets you nothing. I've got 180. It goes up by two points every three months or so. You'll learn all about it when you go to the council,' she added, turning to take her washing upstairs to her room.

My thoughts turned to Mum's horrified face when I'd

optimistically guessed at my chances of being re_
three to six months. My application had after all ,
far back as May, and this was now July. Then
bitterly turned to Sam, enjoying the familiar comfo
of our beautiful home.

'Yes, I've seen them come and go through this p.   ,ean
continued on her return. 'But the housing system's all to hell, I
mean, look at Sonia – only been here six weeks and she's got her
house in East Calder already.' She jabbed the air with her
cigarette. 'It's Donald I'm bloody worried about,' she added,
stabbing an end hard into an ashtray. 'He'll be 16 in October
and, of course there's no men allowed in the refuge and I asked
them what would happen then, and they said, "He can go into a
hostel!" Bloody great, eh?' She shook her head with those last
words, biting her lip with agitation.

'If Sonia's got a house, what's she still doing here?'

'I know. Wouldnae be me, Christ, I'd be out of here the next
day if I'd got a house.'

Some of her bitter frustration seeped through to me and I
tried not to think about it. I had troubles enough of my own.

Jean had her opinions on Sonia's apparent good luck,
including the fact that her father actually worked for the
council. Sonia had been granted permission to stay on at the
refuge until she received her grant which would enable her to
buy household items such as beds, furniture and maybe a
washing machine.

Daily life at the refuge usually meant going out during the
daytime to either shop or to visit the housing department.
There were two large fridge freezers in the outhouse, but with
them being split between four families space was limited. Milk
and fresh bread supplies were essential, which meant a daily trip
to the corner shop.

Since all the women had left their former homes without
being able to pack anything beforehand (and without being able
to retrieve them for a while afterwards either) a lot of clothes
and incidental shopping had to be done too. Debbie always
returned to the refuge struggling with several bags of new
clothes for herself and the children. Debbie and Jean made
frequent trips to the council offices, Debbie to find out how
many points she would be awarded, and Jean to remind them of

he fact that she was still actually waiting for a house.

'I don't care if I make a nuisance of myself, I go up there every week.'

'They'll get so fed up with having to deal with you that they'll give you a house?' I asked.

'Aye. Got nothing to lose, have I?' she said.

My day consisted of being disturbed by Rosie as she wriggled about in the single bed we shared usually around 5 a.m. I'd get dressed hurriedly and quietly pad downstairs with her to make her breakfast and switch on the washing machine. The boys would get up about seven o'clock and we'd enjoy the exclusive use of the living-room while the rest of the house slept on.

The other children didn't appear until after nine, with Billy and Tracey getting their own breakfasts and eating it in front of the television with us. Jade would be next to appear, thumping into the room and plonking herself down in front of the television in a truculent fashion. She refused to answer if I spoke to her and shouted orders and made demands from the other children. She had a fine-featured paleness about her and looked a fragile child despite her apparent need for chaos. Usually friendly towards other children, Rosie preferred not to approach Jade, quite possibly sensing the child's hostility. She frequently carried a rod or a cord ripped from some toy she'd found, intent on whipping everyone and anyone within her reach, squealing appreciatively if one of the children chased her.

On finishing her breakfast, the half empty bowl of cereal would be hurled against the nearest wall, followed by the satisfying twang of the spoon as it bounced off the plasterboard. Jamie inevitably tried to emulate her sister but thankfully, owing to her age, was less abusive. I spoke to and treated the girls the same as the other children, not showing any reaction to bad behaviour or to their constant swearing. When Sonia was present, Jade remained a diluted form of herself, electing not to call anyone 'a fat shite!' until after her mother had left the room.

Once the last adult had moved herself into either the kitchen or the bathroom, I'd set about doing my allotted chores. With everything done by 10 a.m., I'd be ready to go out for the day. The evening meal would be cooked on a first-come first-served basis with, say, two women being able to use the cooker and microwave between them. Nothing was in short supply and the kitchen was fully fitted and modern. Cups remained scarce, but only because the children broke them, either by accident or otherwise. If something was needed, say a new tin opener or a mop, one could buy it for the refuge and have the money refunded by one of the workers.

At night, Debbie and Sonia would sit in one of their bedrooms talking endlessly while Jean had the luxury of her own television in her bedroom. This meant I was the only adult trying to watch something while the rest of the children screamed around me. My children were the only ones to be in their beds by 9 p.m. At about 10 p.m., Debbie or Sonia would return to the kitchen to make chips or bacon rolls for supper. The other children, including two-year-old Jamie, stayed up, ran about, playing or fighting loudly until 1 a.m. or 2 a.m. The teenagers rarely sat with us, with Donald and Claire staying in their own room and Damen often staying the night with his own friends.

For the first three nights or so, one of the refuge workers in the office would phone to talk with me. They'd ask how I was feeling and about any problems I might want to discuss with them about the refuge. I asked them about going back to my home to collect more clothes and items for the kids, and a firm date was made for the Thursday.

Sam had phoned the office that day, demanding the immediate return of his daughter. Although he hadn't been abusive towards them, they had noted his controlled, very clipped tone of voice.

'We've set a time for the police to come too, so that'll be two of us, two policemen and you,' Irma detailed efficiently. I recognised her voice as the one that I'd had to phone the morning that we'd escaped. 'Do you think you can handle it, Susan?'

'Yeah, I think so,' I lied, sounding light and indifferent to the task ahead. I made a rough list of items starting with the most needed at the top. Rosie's buggy, her nappies and more clothes for her. Clothes for the boys, their shoes, coats and some toys. Medication for Ryan and me and clothes for me.

Come the day, I felt nervous with a sense of foreboding about the trip. The workers appeared on time, driving a blue van. It was the two women whom I'd met the year before, Wanda and

Frances, the ones who had given me John Hanrahan's name.

Debbie had offered to look after the children, and the boys were looking forward to my bringing back some familiar toys and books they'd requested. My thoughts were filled with Sam's red angry face greeting me at the door, and my heart thumped harder. As the van's large side door slid shut beside me, I consoled my worried mind with thoughts of being able to see my home once more.

On sight of my street dark feelings of homesickness settled within me every time I spotted something familiar. The expected police car wasn't there yet, so Wanda parked the van at the top of the road which was five doors away from our house. 'So what does John say about getting your husband out of the house, or are you not going to bother?' Frances asked, turning awkwardly in her seat to talk to me.

'Well, John doesn't think we'd have much luck getting him out through the courts, and anyway, according to Jean and Debbie, I'd have to take out some sort of interdict to keep him away.' Both women nodded, still gazing towards the house.

'I don't think I could do it either, I'd be a prisoner in my own home,' I added resignedly. 'Jean pointed out that it could take Sam less than a minute to break into the house, to stand winking at the police telling them that I'd willingly let him in. It's more bother than it's worth.'

'If you asked him to let you have the house, would he let you?' Wanda asked.

'I wouldn't go back,' my voice was lowering along with my spirits. Just hearing the words out loud, underlined how blatantly awful my situation was.

'Yeah, at least he doesn't know where you are this way,' Frances agreed, as a police car made it's way slowly towards us. Both women waved, pointing towards the house and started up the van to follow them.

The street was deserted as usual, and we stood awkwardly together, watching Frances unfurl several black bags from a roll she had and handing them to Wanda. I hurriedly detailed Sam's expected reaction to our plans, while the policemen aimlessly scanned the windows for signs of life. 'He won't co-operate, and although he's six feet four inches and weighs 22 stones he's quick on his feet.'

'Now if he's in,' one officer said, 'and he refuses us all entry, which he can do, you'll have to decide whether to go in yourself or to just leave things till later.'

I shook my head in disgust at the law they must adhere to. The police had been asked to attend, presumably to deter any violence towards us, and to stop any damage I might have in mind to Sam's property. This was no lover's tiff, they knew I was at a battered women's refuge and I was not returning with them for the opportunity to patch things up either. Yet he explained that they could be forced to stand on the doorstep, respecting Sam's rights while I was left alone with my 'allegedly' violent husband to retrieve much-needed belongings. Everything's going his way, I thought bitterly.

I tried the door handle, and it was locked. 'He's out,' I shouted back to the group with obvious relief, and jammed my key into the lock to open the door.

CHAPTER ELEVEN

Monday, 17 July

My house, my beautiful house. Everything was as I had left it last Monday morning. He hadn't even done the dishes. 'You'll get rehoused?' one of the policemen asked as he watched me diving around the living-room collecting things. He raised his eyebrows when I told him I'd be lucky if it was within a year. Items were piled up in the hall, as Wanda wanted to stay by the door being 'lookout'. Frances based herself in the kitchen. She'd found the pantry cupboard and was shouting out the contents which included medicines.

'Calpol and cream!' she'd shout.

'Aye.'

'Box of inhaler discs!'

'Aye, there should be two.'

Upstairs, dragging a half full black bag behind me, I tried to clear Rosie's chest of drawers. Into the boys' room, and everything seemed to be on the floor, their shoes, coats, jogging bottoms etc.

I scanned the floor for the toy on David's list, but had to settle for one or two play figures and a transformer thing. In the bathroom I grabbed our toothbrushes, taking Sam's and impulsively throwing it head first into the toilet bowl. The officers were still downstairs, making me think of the opportunity for destruction. I considered scribbling across the walls in lipstick 'Laugh now, wifebeating bastard!' Pour water onto his side of the mattress, and cut the legs off the trousers I'd pressed for him only the week before. But I stood at the door, wheezing slightly, and walked over to the window

112

instead. My house, my beautiful house. It's not fair. I wanted to stay, I didn't want to go back. And Sam, what were his thoughts? Remorse, regret maybe? Aye, right.

Back in the living-room and seeing how agitated I was, one officer urged me to take my time. He pointed out the group photographs of the kids which I piled into another black bag. In the kitchen, my beautiful kitchen, I took as many of our cups as was possible for the refuge. Frances suggested a rake through the freezer for food that we could eat. I didn't even look at the garden. I couldn't have . . . I would've cried . . .

At the refuge I waited constantly for news from John. Sam was not prepared to move out of our home, and he wanted full custody of Rosie. I mentally berated myself for thinking that he might see sense and at least let me have custody. But no, that wasn't his way, not when we were together, and definitely not now we were apart. Why should he feel obliged to move out of the family home so that his family could move back in when his revenge could be so freely exercised? He'd have no qualms about rattling around a three-bedroomed house, while his family managed in a woman's refuge with four other families. It was my choice to leave, of course, no one forced me to go.

In the meantime, he requested access on a residential basis every weekend. That meant no weekends together as a family, and less contact with her brothers once they returned to school. The sheriff, after hearing John plead my case, gave me interim custody of the children. He allowed Sam one residential weekend out of two with Rosie, and a three-hour access on the intervening weekend. Sam had no interest in seeing David or Ryan, and their relief was obvious.

The court's decision sounded fair to me and John informed me that this was how access would operate until our day in court to settle custody.

Despite the overwhelming hateful feelings I had for Sam, I stood by my 'Separation Speech' and had no wish to stop him seeing his daughter. The Interlocutor also made provision for a holiday week for Sam and Rosie, which he could take whenever he wanted. The boys were horrified and looked upon the decree as a reward to Sam, despite his bad behaviour.

'Did John tell that Sheriff where we are, what that git's like?'

Ryan clenched his fists, his face clouding over. 'He'll shout at her, Mum, she'll never manage for all that time.'

'Just say no!' David demanded, slicing the air with a flat palm.

Explaining that Rosie still loved, and possibly missed, her Daddy didn't seem to help. The fact that Sam could continue to be as obstructive and petty as he liked, and would still be able to have Rosie, seemed to overwhelm their sense of what is fair and right in their world.

Whispers of guilt entered my thoughts, forcing me to examine past events. Why didn't I ever call the police when he'd assaulted me? Their reports could have helped me now. He could have been ordered to leave the house by the courts and at least the children would have had familiar surroundings to comfort them. Why had I left it so late to apply for housing? Why didn't I do as Wanda had advised all those months before?

Life at the refuge meant no restrictions of previous family life, and with the children on holidays I concentrated on them and their activities. I encouraged them to play with Debbie's kids and took them all for walks around the area for something to do. I dotted the day with odd treats, and at night, while Rosie slept soundly in the bed we shared, both boys would listen intently to updates on the custody and house fronts.

I had decided to be honest about everything, and for them to be included in my attempts to keep the family together, and they knew that Sam was going for full custody of their sister. They also knew that we couldn't stay with Nana, because we'd be badly overcrowded, which wouldn't look good for our custody bid.

We'd discuss any worries or problems they had, with David's main concern being that they were unable to stay at their beloved primary school. We were halfway through the summer holidays, and although I too dreaded the thought of having to move them, I lightly dissuaded him from thinking about it until nearer the time.

Ryan missed his Nana, had started biting his nails and worried incessantly about Rosie having to stay with Sam. The first residential weekend had been set, and he'd interrupt his play to be reminded of the details and times she'd be returned to us. He whispered to me of his suspicions that Sam really didn't 'want Rosie', he merely wanted to deprive us of her.

I wrote a letter to Marjery, and in it I explained where we were and why we had to leave, since there was every possibility that she didn't know. My relationship with her during the past five years had maintained a forced air of respect. I made a conscious effort to do what was expected of me and more, and if she had cause to criticise me even once throughout our relationship, she successfully kept it to herself.

Marjery believed that marriage was for life and that you stood by your man regardless of his behaviour. Her underlying belief was that if a marriage broke up, it was because of the wife. Her theory was explained to me during various occasions, and she remained closed to any suggestion that her philosophy might be flawed.

She believed that if the husband went with other women, it was because he'd lacked the appropriate attention from his wife. If he drank away the week's wages, it was up to the wife to get a job/salt away some money/get him to stop. If he battered her, then she should stop doing whatever it was that annoyed him so much.

Her attitude amazed me and her small-minded opinions of such matters obviously gave me an insight into her son's thought patterns. Marjery believed that her marriage survived the 25 years that it did because of her efforts. She was possibly right. Little consideration was ever given to the woman in a relationship. She was a woman, and she had coped. Why couldn't they?

Now that I had left her son, his side of events would be conveniently watered down, ensuring the finished painting depicted me as the spiteful, unpredictable madam that Linda had been before me.

I assured her that the children were fine and that because of Sam's bitter pettiness it was unlikely that she'd ever see the boys again. I thanked her for her efforts to include them within her family, and added that I'd appreciated the interest and time she'd given them, when their real Gran (Keith's Mum) had ignored their very existence.

I apologised for the disappointment she must feel at our separation. I admitted to nothing that could fuel her opinions about me and my role as a wife. I wished her well for the future, making sure she realised that I'd be willing to keep in touch, for the sake of the children if nothing else. It was a carefully constructed note, however, as there was the very real chance that she'd snort loudly at my attempt to keep her informed and hand it to her loving son, who had been cruelly wronged by his bitter wife. Her loyalty towards her four precious sons was legendary, and sadly wasted on them.

Being at the refuge hadn't improved my personal well being, as was usually the case when women like me had escaped such stressful lives at home. I hardly ate. I lost more weight, signalled by the lycra ski pants I wore beginning to fall down. While the other women smoked, I bit my nails and picked at rough skin on my hands constantly. The pressure on my neck muscles gave me headaches, but like a child my hands were a definite comfort in my mouth. Flashbacks continued to sieze any idle time I had before trying to get to sleep and I'd fantasise about vengeful attacks on Sam. My dreams were vivid and eventful and I'd often be awake before Rosie began her morning wriggling session at 5 a.m.

The women sang and danced to loud music on Debbie's ghettoblaster, which was permanently switched on in the kitchen. Whenever I passed it, I'd turn down the volume slightly. Whenever they passed it, they'd turn it up, cheerfully mouthing the words to the latest beat. They could laugh and joke about their situation, singing on their way to the shower:

'I'm gonna wash that Bas-tard outta' my hair,
I'm gonna wash that Bas-tard outta' my hair,
An' then I'll kick that Bas-tard right doon the stair
and send him off to jai-ll!'

Saturday, 21 July
We're staying at Mum's tonight and Rosie is away. Mum hired a transit van, informing Sam first of her intentions to collect the boys' bikes, toys and beds. The operation went successfully with Sam showing no objection. She thought he looked incredibly stressed, averting his eyes from her and sweating profusely. When Mum had mentioned that she'd at least keep in touch with him until he moved, his sarcastic response numbed her into silence. 'Is that what she thinks?' he'd sneered. 'Well, you can tell her that I will *not* be moving out of this house, and she will definitely not be moving in.'

116

She'd taken Rosie up with her, five hours before the agreed hour, but we appreciate he'll stick to the 6 p.m. Sunday return time. I miss her terribly. I actually ache for her.

Nobody thinks Sam will gain custody, but I live, eat and sleep with the thought of losing her. It's another worry I can do without. He will indeed have punished me if he gets her.

Mum is stressed and mortified that her daughter is in a women's refuge. She hates not being able to see us every day. May generously keeps her company, listens to her and supports Mum's decision to put her beautiful cottage up for a council exchange. The first advert goes into the local paper next week, and she's optimistic about the response from people tired of keeping their large family houses clean and of waiting on council transfer lists for a pensioner's cottage such as Mum's. It's a good plan which could get us out of here and I appreciate the sacrifice, possibly more than she'll ever know . . .

Another addition to the refuge arrived in the shape of Linda and her two babies, from Glasgow. Charlotte, another worker had brought her, and while Debbie and Sonia chatted with Linda and took turns at holding the younger baby, Charlotte took time to ask how I was coping so far.

I said I thought everything was as well as could be expected, with my main problem being that I was having difficulty in presenting myself homeless to the council. I'd been advised to walk into the Housing Office during business hours to be given an appointment to see the Housing Officer. I would officially present myself as homeless, answer all her questions and in time be awarded points in writing. This would then give me an indication of just how long we'd need to wait before being offered a tenancy. In practice however, being homeless was no guarantee to getting an appointment with the appropriate officer.

'She'th not available today,' the teenage receptionist behind the counter politely lisped. And on another day, 'She'th theeing clienths until 5 p.m., maybe you could call back tomorrow?'

'Oh sure, there's no hurry right enough,' I'd reply sarcastically whilst herding the children out of the queue.

Charlotte tutted irritably at my failed attempts to get onto 'the list'. She assured me that she'd phone them to complain, and to demand an appointment be made for me over the phone.

Meanwhile, our numbers in the house swelled to 17, with every bedroom now housing a family.

Linda's background was similar to Sonia's who had also lived with a boyfriend who indulged in drugs and the party scene. Like Debbie she'd come this far from her home city to get away from her partner, and expected him to find her at any moment. Her children, 15-month-old Kyle and baby Stephanie, were both in nappies, and both feeding on milk bottles. Linda was long haired and slim, about 22 and seemed immediately attracted to Sonia and Debbie.

The threesome would sit for hours smoking and talking while their children ran riot around the house. Observing this clan of women drawn together through similar circumstance became a diversion to my own pressing problems. Their main topics of conversation centred on being rehoused, and men.

Sonia and Debbie already had new boyfriends, and lived for the weekend when they could go out. Like anxious teenagers, they discussed their clothes, brushed and put up each other's hair in different styles and swapped make-up and tips.

Only Sonia and I had family members who were willing to support us in our plight. Had Mum's house been big enough I certainly would have stayed with her, whereas Sonia seemed to loathe any time spent with her reasonably well-off parents and refused to move in with them.

She was a 'Goth' and dressed permanently in black, including her favourite black Doc Marten boots. Her ears were adorned with several studs, originally silver, now blackened with age. She had a spotty, grubby complexion and her hair was as red as the dye she used almost weekly.

I'd never thought about how I presented myself to other people before then, but had concluded that their collective impression of me was one of being mature if not matronly. Certainly not one of them.

I never commented on Sonia's appearance (nor anyone else's) yet she felt the instant need to justify her dress sense and way of life to me, which always included the love and future hopes she had for her girls. Her parents 'fussed too much, expected too much and suggested too much', and she dreaded having to attend the Sunday dinners her mother invited them to, which often deteriorated into screaming matches.

Moreover, her newly allocated council house was only one street away from her parents, and she anticipated much interference from her mother.

Jean's mother loved and supported her, but had sadly died leaving Jean with no family network to turn to.

Linda's large family seemed willing to help. However, she knew from past experience that seeking refuge in one of their homes would mean eventually attracting her maniac boyfriend's unwanted attentions. The refuge system was her only practical means of escape but she was hopeful of returning to her home town to be housed eventually.

Debbie also came from a large family and confessed to little contact with her parents. At 31, she still dressed her curvy frame like a teenager and wore cropped jackets and tight leggings complete with high-heeled shoes for everyday wear. She propped her curly hair up in a girlish pony tail which swung gaily behind her as she teetered along on enormous Cuban heels.

'I reckon I'm the daughter my Mum forgets she has,' she told me once. 'I've learnt to live with it,' she added indifferently.

They borrowed extensively from each other's bedrooms, lending money and freely trusted each other to oversee their children. They spent forever on the phone, although they insisted they hadn't given out the secret refuge phone number to anyone. This particularly annoyed Jean, since she was certain that the refuge workers would find out. It was a punishable offence to have friends and family phone the refuge, and the workers' threat to any abuse of this rule was to have the phone switched off.

'When folk come in here, they're so bloody grateful and they think it's a great organisation,' Jean quietly explained to me once. 'Then they get all petty about the rules and regulations and they start breaking them, and moan about the place being like a prison.'

On entering the refuge, women were given a list of the rules, obviously introduced to make the communal style of living easier.

We all knew that Debbie and Sonia received calls from male and female callers every day yet we realised that if the workers found out, we'd all be penalised by the phone's disconnection.

We were warned not to doubt this threat. Jean had experience of previous residents' abuses being found out, and the phone was indeed cut off for a while.

We all knew that Sonia arranged to meet her abusive former partner at least once a week. That she allowed him two or three hours unofficial access to the girls while she shopped, and that he accompanied her on the bus to the stop before the refuge even, but I was urged never to mention it to any of the workers by Debbie.

'So what if she does meet her ex once a week?' I answered, more amazed at such an amicable arrangement. Something my petty, bitter and twisted husband would never consider.

'Because she'd get kicked out if they knew,' she hissed. 'We're supposed to be too scared to live with them, and if they're civil enough to see the children they're civil enough to move out of the house and give it to the wife and family.'

'I suppose there's a few who leave the man, go into a refuge for a few months, get another, better house maybe and . . .'

'Aye, and he moves into their nice new house with her.'

We both nodded knowingly.

'Nobody likes to be conned right enough,' she added, pulling at her stretch T-shirt in an attempt to cover her cleavage. Despite Sonia having a house to go to now, she still didn't want to lose her friend through my loose mouth. Although she and Sonia must have been aware of the possible danger their constant bending of the rules put the rest of us in, they carried on regardless, safe in the knowledge that they'd never be found out.

They never threatened me or Jean, who could get on with them far better than I ever could. But as a pair, obviously intent on doing what they wanted, they presented a formidable force. Without even mentioning the consequences of telling the workers, I knew that neither Jean nor I wanted to find ourselves on the wrong side of them. These people weren't our neighbours or work colleagues who could be forgotten over a weekend. We lived with them. Now that there were three like-minded souls under the same roof, it made things that little bit harder.

On the other hand, the refuge workers had been known to spot-check the house at odd hours during the night or day, and such stories from Jean kept the threesome on their toes. However, apart from workers bringing another woman to stay at the refuge, there were never any checks made during my entire time in the refuge system.

Monday, 24 July
I've been up since 6 a.m. – done the chores we are all supposed to do. I've walked into town, done a shopping, come back, made lunch and it's only 12.30!

We've to suffer Jade all day since it looks as if Sonia's staying in. Both girls woke every two hours last night screaming for their Mum, who didn't turn up until 9.30 a.m. this morning! I remember her once telling me 'all I care about is that my children are happy'. What crap!

Debbie was supposed to be looking after them, but obviously doesn't hear them running around the house screeching at the tops of their voices . . .

Although it had happened before, I'd presumed that Sonia was merely failing in her attempt at putting her brood to bed quietly. They woke me, despite my earplugs (a legacy from years of suffering Sam's snoring), and eventually the boys were jolted from their sleep at the panicked cries downstairs.

We'd lie awake talking quietly, while listening to the girls' constant wailing, their thin voices shouting out 'Mummy, Mummy' over and over and with no answer.

'Doesn't Sonia hear them?' Ryan whined, wanting to drift back to sleep.

'They're maybe having nightmares,' I offered, which backed up the girls' destructive behaviour during the day.

But after watching these women with their children, it came as no surprise that Sonia wouldn't hear them. Sonia's children were not so much a part of her as attached to her. Once engaged in conversation the girls became a disruptive distraction she did her best to ignore. Communication between mother and child was at the very minimum, with actual eye contact hardly being achieved throughout an entire day.

An example would be the time I happened to be in the living-room with the others one late afternoon. David and Tracey were colouring in a book together, Ryan and Billy played happily in the garden, while Jade assaulted them with a treasured stick she'd found.

Jamie was thirsty and approached Sonia to ask for a drink. At only 22 months her speech was limited, but when she asked for the 'clink' the first time, Sonia was talking to Debbie, Jean and me and she ignored the child completely. Fifteen minutes later, Jamie was still thirsty and had asked for a drink maybe five or six times by then. Sonia continued to talk, not even lowering her head to look at Jamie, who was now clambering up onto her mother's knees as she sat on the couch.

Jamie changed her tone to a continuous whine while Sonia, now listening to something Jean was saying, lifted her head above Jamie's to hear. Over and over and over, the child asked the same question, even attempting to place chubby hands onto her mother's cheeks to gain her attention.

I willed Sonia to answer Jamie, my heart increasing its beat with anger at the scene, but she merely swiped at Jamie's hands as one would swipe at a passing fly. Jean stopped talking to allow Sonia to hear Jamie, who was now beginning to cry. She rubbed her eyes and sat silent for a moment, contemplating a pen mark she'd discovered on her jeans before eventually struggling to stand on her mother's knees. But Sonia had decided she'd had enough of Jamie's weight and promptly lifted her up and plonked her onto the carpet beside the couch. She continued talking to us, Jamie continued repeating her question.

'The bairn wants a drink, hen!' Jean blurted in exaggerated fashion, as if joking with Sonia. It had been nearly 45 minutes since the child's first request.

'Aye, I'll get you a drink hen . . . ' she said quietly, glancing at Jamie now lying prone and sobbing beside her feet, before continuing the sentence that Jean had interrupted. She made no attempt to move and reached for her lighter to start another cigarette. At that point I had to get up to leave the room.

There was no consideration of her children, and no interest in them whatsoever. She often had no idea where they were, and as long as she could sit and talk, she had no intention of checking on their welfare. I never heard her talking to them, actually telling them anything, she only asked questions. 'Did you hit Billy?' or 'Why did you do that?' or 'Where is Tracey's pen, Jade?'

She disciplined Jade by shouting, grabbing and pulling the child to attention, and that was only when she could catch her. She refrained from actually hitting her whenever I was present although I fully expected her to.

The most tragic happenings would be when Sonia was preparing herself for a night out. The signal would go up when Jamie noticed her mum applying various shades of grey make-up to her face. Jade already knew the score, and her behaviour would triple in intensity. 'Don't go to the shop Mummy, don't go to the shop,' Jade would plead.

'Have to darling . . . don't do that . . !'

'Debbie go to the shop Mummy.'

'No, no, I'll go,' she said, continuing to stare into her hand mirror. 'Bring back sweets!' she added.

'Don't want sweeeets . . .' Jade sobbed punching at her mother's arm.

By the time the taxi had arrived both girls were screaming hysterically in the kitchen clutching pathetically at Sonia's legs as she elegantly smoked a final cigarette.

Both girls raised their arms to be lifted, and eventually Sonia relented and picked up one of them. 'Please not go to the shop, pleeease . . . pleeeease . . .'

Jamie clung to Sonia's neck, with Jade weeping uncontrollably into Sonia's skirt. Debbie would peel the baby's hands from her mother's reddened neck with Sonia preening her hair without even a backward glance at the girls. She'd gratefully squeeze herself outside while Debbie attempted to calm two bawling, ferocious beings, left squirming in some frustrated frenzy on the kitchen floor.

When sleep came, their nights without Sonia were continuously broken with periods of wandering around the darkened house calling out for her. Amazingly Debbie and her entire family never heard them thumping and screaming during the night, despite their bedroom being downstairs, and neither did Linda.

I'd mention it the next day, with Debbie denying any knowledge of the girls having been up during the night. I think there was one night when she did hear them and she'd soothed them back to sleep.

Once my children were awake, I decided not to approach the

girls myself. Jade took no instruction from me anyway, and the situation angered me. I hated Sonia for our combined suffering, her girls and ours, because nothing would stop her enjoying herself.

No wonder she was delaying the move into her own house. She knew she was on to a good thing with Debbie as resident babysitter.

Another of the refuge's rules was that no one was to be left babysitting more than four children and that included their own. Debbie barely scraped past that one and not through design either. Thankfully Damen preferred to stay with his own friends on weekend nights. However, staying overnight anywhere without your children was not allowed.

I often wished the workers would make one of their famous visits one morning and discover Sonia's absence. She'd arrive back around 10 a.m. with a bag full of sweets for the girls and immediately engross herself in a debriefing session with Debbie and Linda.

CHAPTER TWELVE

Debbie's relationship with her kids was an improvement on Sonia's but this was probably because of their ages. Damen at 13 was firmly entrenched in teenage culture, mood and mode of communication. He stayed in their bedroom listening to music and watching television, with brief silent sightings of him in the kitchen being the norm. Debbie could and would talk to her children though. She had a no-nonsense bossy attitude with them that no one challenged.

Despite suffering 15 years with her partner, they'd never married. This meant that she was the legal guardian of their children and when finally leaving the family home, she'd severed all contact with him. She had no lawyer, and even kept her location a secret from some family she had living nearby – to ensure her chances of staying undetected. He was looking for her though, and Debbie knew that she would 'be mincemeat' if he did find them.

Tracey aged eight and Billy aged ten knew how to play and were likeable and friendly kids. Although they rarely approached Debbie when she was talking with Sonia and Linda, they were at least assured of their mum's attention if they did ask a question. As a family they ate constantly, with their main diet consisting of chips and hamburgers, chips and sausages, chips and egg. Everything came out of a tin or microwave dish with the exception of potatoes for the chips which were fried conventionally on the cooker top. If any of the children was thirsty, it had to be juice, either diluted or fizzy. Drinking milk or water was out of the question and they marvelled at Rosie's acceptance of a cup of water from the tap once. They bickered and argued with each other like any other family, and received single slaps from Debbie as discipline. She made no attempt to entertain them, only ever taking them out to shop.

Debbie also stayed out with her new boyfriend overnight, but since her children were much older she knew they'd cope better than Sonia's two.

Billy and Tracey dodged and ducked their way out of various assaults by Jade and would often be hurt to the point of tears. However, Debbie left Jade's discipline to her pal without comment.

Linda's babies, 15-month-old Kyle and three-month-old Stephanie, were plainly too young to be noticeable. Kyle spent his days rolling his milk bottle up the stairs in a determined effort to climb to the top. Linda found comfort in the clique that dominated the refuge, and because of this there wasn't much opportunity to speak to her myself.

Again there seemed to be little interest in her children. Kyle was allowed to wander the house without check but, because of his age, he naturally went back to her for top-ups to his juice beaker and for biscuits and unlike Sonia, she would almost immediately fetch him what he wanted. Linda told us that her boyfriend was the nicest guy anyone would wish to meet and that it was drugs that turned him into an enraged animal, intent on smashing her head through the nearest window he could find. She was sure that if there was a place on this earth without drugs, then he'd never lift a finger to her again.

When she'd finally decided to leave him, she'd returned to their flat to collect some clothes, taking a neighbour with her for support. Once inside though, he'd pushed her friend outside and slammed the door, and viciously attacked Linda in the hall in a frenzy of kicks and punches. The neighbour had witnessed all this through the letterbox and had stayed long enough to help Linda once she had managed to escape her latest and last beating, but the police had decided that there was little that they could do. Linda's one witness, with her view from the letterbox, was just not enough evidence to secure a conviction, but she could press charges anyway.

Both Sonia and Debbie took turns in giving Linda's baby Stephanie her bottle, the novelty rekindling any memories they had of their own babies. They'd eagerly volunteer to watch Linda's children while she dived out to the local shop, and in return she'd often take Tracey into town with her.

Stephanie, however, would spend long periods of time just lying on the rug on the floor, while the women talked. Despite being awake and active she'd have nothing to look at but the ceiling and when she tired of this, it was assumed that she must be either wet, tired or just hungry. Linda made no attempt to play with her or with Kyle. There were no songs sung, no stories told and no games invented for any of the children of the threesome. The children were there to be serviced, kept reasonably clean and fed, anything else was a veritable chore. For their part, they had to 'go and play' – that was all that their mothers asked.

I answered the phone one morning and it was Frances from the office warning us about another addition to the refuge due that day. 'I know the refuge is full, Susan, but I was wondering if one of you could squeeze this woman in beside you somewhere.'

'Well, I'm pretty full up but maybe Jean could help I suppose. But it'll depend on what she's like really.'

'Oh, I don't think she'll be any bother. She's middle aged, very upset and seems a quiet type . . . nice woman. But the other refuge only has two young families in it, and they're out all the time and I really feel that she needs company if nothing else. She's on her own, her kids are all grown up,' she enthused, as if selling something.

'Well, I'll mention it to everyone, I'm sure we could fit her in,' I lied. I wasn't keen on another arrival and already felt that the house was bursting at its ragged seams anyway, but it wasn't my house or my place to object.

'Why don't they get Sonia to move into her own bloody place if they're so short of space?' I complained to Jean. 'Christ, it's hardly as if they're throwing her out onto the street is it?'

'Jesus,' Jean said, ignoring my question. 'Wonder what this one's story is, eh? At least we're only approaching middle age and we've broken free. Imagine being middle aged and still getting slapped around the house?'

Margaret was a nice woman. Debbie and I were the only ones still in when Helen, yet another worker, arrived with Margaret trailing pitifully behind. Helen sat alone on one of the couches talking non-stop about her holiday in Amsterdam while Margaret wept silent tears that rolled continuously down her fat, freckled cheeks.

She was in her early 50s and heavy set and seemed gentle in nature, but had suffered immense stress over the past 48 hours due to her man's recent mental problems. After 26 years of marriage her husband had become paranoid that his wife was committing adultery with various men. Even a glance in a male neighbour's direction would send him into an anxiety attack that saw him watching her every move.

During the last days in the house with him, she'd been sleeping on the couch in her living-room. He set his alarm to go off at hourly intervals during the night so that he could check on her, making sure she was still there. Between that and his constant accusations about her bedding every man that existed, she entered the refuge for a much-needed break. Her family of five were too accessible for him, and again some of her kids found it hard to believe her claims about their beloved Dad.

'I mean, look at me. I'd say to him, "I'm not 21 any more, Jim. I'm old and fat and hardly any bloody catch," I'd say, but he wouldn't listen. He'd just bring his face up close to mine and spit at me in disgust . . .' she trailed off with a sob.

Saturday, 29 July

I wish I could die. I wish I could die. If I could die now, Fatso would get Rosie, Mum could have the boys. There would be no more horrendous pressures on them, no more violence for them to see. Mum wouldn't be frantically looking for an exchange every hour of every day and no one would be hurt any more.

Debbie punched me yesterday morning. I wanted to hit her back, God I wanted to, but I immediately thought, 'Good, she'll be evicted!' and I walked away. Afterwards, she laughed about it, giggling nervously with her family who had watched it happen and with her friend whose child we were fighting over. Sonia had left her kids overnight again, and Jamie was running around the house screaming for nearly an hour that night.

Totally fed up with the situation, and the kids were awake of course, I went downstairs and battered on Debbie's bedroom door shouting at her to get up. She was furious – she'd gotten a fright, and she was totally pissed off that I'd actually spoken to her like that. It was 3 a.m.

I waited all morning for Debbie to get up. I couldn't sleep the whole night I was so bloody angry about it and at 10 a.m. Sonia returned to hear Margaret and me telling her what had happened. 'Oh well,' she sighed, 'that's the end of my nights out then.' She went to speak to Debbie, who got up and came storming into the living-room and started shouting at me about waking her children the way I had that night. I stood my ground, screaming back.

There were seven children who saw her smack the side of my face, and of course Sonia too.

'What did you hit me for?' I roared into her face. We were eyeball to eyeball. '

"Cos you woke ma bairns,' she spat back.

'Well, you woke mine up, so I'm allowed to punch you back, am I?' I lifted my fist up.

'You try it and I'll rip yer fuckin' head off!'

It was Frances who took my call about the assault. Debbie's punch hadn't hurt me physically, but the shock and the humiliation I felt was overwhelming. Frances listened to my side of the story, waiting patiently for me to weep into the mouthpiece as the dreaded flashback returned with a vengeance. She informed me that the incident would be thoroughly investigated and that Debbie would probably be evicted.

Ryan stood beside me as I crouched by the phone, his hand patting my shoulder in his attempt to comfort me. On the bus journey to Mum's I'd assured the boys that Debbie would be evicted now, that the rules of the refuge did not tolerate violence between residents.

'Where will they go?' David asked.

'Who cares! She should've thought about that before she whacked me,' I ranted.

Luckily, I'd just taken Rosie upstairs for a morning nap so she hadn't been there to witness the incident unlike the boys who remained white-faced and sullen.

Now the revelations about the threesome's behaviour had to be brought out for examination. I told Frances all about Sonia and Debbie's catalogue of abuses. She didn't sound surprised, and assured me that she'd call me back and keep me informed. Before ringing off, she asked if I wanted to involve the police and press charges.

'Well, I think I should, but really I reckon Sonia will just deny anything happened and she'll get off with it.'

'Well, it's up to you, Susan. Are there no bruises or scratches on your face, you know, to back you up?'

'No.'

My thoughts were scattered and disturbed. I needed guidance and asked Frances her opinion. 'It's up to you, really, you're entitled to press charges,' she said, 'I can't say more than that.'

This was the day that Rosie was to leave us for her week's holiday with Sam. We were all dreading it and had arranged to stay the night at Mum's anyway, giving us a thankful break from the refuge even before the assault. I packed her bag with her clothes, favourite cuddly toy, toothbrush and dummy which she still used to soothe her to sleep.

When Frances called back, she sounded officious and detached. 'We're at the refuge now, and Sonia and Debbie both deny you were slapped.' There was a moment's silence before I realised she was awaiting my answer.

'Well, what did you expect them to say for Christ's sake – "Oh, yes, I slapped her, I'll just pack my things?"' My sarcasm was obvious and she laboured a sigh. 'I suppose they denied ever leaving the kids and staying out all bloody night as well, eh?'

'No, Sonia's admitted to that – but then, of course, Margaret could vouch for that one.'

'Well, my kids were there, Christ everyone's kids were there . . . I don't suppose Margaret heard anything?' I asked hopefully. I couldn't believe they were doubting my word.

'Margaret says she was in the shower, she heard nothing.'

This was true, Margaret had been heading for the shower just after Sonia arrived back.

'Look, Frances, I'm telling the truth. I'm not going to make something like this up for nothing, am I?'

'Well, this is what we're trying to work out. Look, Wanda and I think it would be a good idea if you came back to the refuge for a chat with them . . .'

'No bloody way!' I nearly shouted.

'I think it would help.'

'Frances, Sonia and Debbie are not the type to talk things through and I'm bloody sure I'll not be shaking hands with them either. I stood in the way of their cosy little babysitting racket and

I had to be put in my place. Christ, don't you realise that's why Sonia was so reluctant to move into her house?' There was silence again while Frances considered her next suggestion.

'Well, if you won't come down to talk with them, then there's little we can do,' she said.

'So you're not going to move Debbie?'

'Well, we've no proof that she hit you, have we? Look, why don't you stay at your Mum's for the weekend and when it's time for you to come back, we'll be here to meet you.'

'Frances, you must be joking,' I gasped into the mouthpiece. 'Debbie assaults me, gets a sympathetic pat on the back from you because Sonia's her witness, and I move back in for some more abuse from the two of them because they know you'll never believe me anyway? Come on!' The whole conversation was becoming farcical.

'Right, just stay on at your Mum's till Monday, and then we'll arrange to move you to our other safe house.' The word 'safe' seemed comical.

'Is there no chance of moving Debbie then?'

'Not with the way things have happened, no.'

Monday, 31 July 1995

The police will do nothing. The refuge will do nothing. Frances called this morning to confirm them moving me to refuge two. It's in another town, well off anything remotely like a beaten track. She told me that the workers had agreed that I wasn't lying about the incident. So what! Don't suppose they asked Debbie to move, it's easier to ask me, a quiet wee woman, with no visible spine. I'll just uproot my family again and just go. Tomorrow I must return to the refuge to collect my things (they won't do it for me). I mean, that just tops the list for humiliation eh? I bet they're laughing so hard right now Debbie and Sonia – glad to be rid of me. I was wrong again. I wanted a decent night's sleep and I get thrown out and resettled.

The wrong decision, another disastrous bloody choice. Stupid, stupid, fucking stupid cow that I am. Should've known that none of this would go your way – fucking idiot that you are. Why didn't you smack her back? Why didn't you rip her fucking black hair out by the rotten roots? Her children now see that what their mother has been teaching them all their miserable little lives was right! Do wrong and you will *always* get away with it! If you don't get your way hit someone. Lie and *nothing* will happen to you!

My children wonder how their Mum did nothing wrong yet she gets punished for it! After all, their step-father did it to her and now the rest of the fucking world does it to her too! What they must think of me.

I feel so angry, so let down, so stupid, so fucking stupid. My throat aches, I just want to cry all the time. I wish I could die. Rosie wouldn't miss me, the boys' lives would be greatly improved without 'stupidworks' here stumbling about with their innocent little lives. Why can't I just go to sleep and not wake up?

The policewoman diligently wrote down my side of events, while the boys played noisily outside. It was an actual embarrassment to me to have to admit my situation, and to the latest calamity to befall me. 'Just as well I joined the Lucky White Heather Club?' I said, forcing a smile at the irony of it all. Inside I felt chewed up and hopeless. Bad enough that I had to go into a refuge, and bad enough that I be assaulted while I'm there. But worse, far worse than all that was the fact that no one believed my side of events and no one would do anything about it. Just as it was with Sam, they'd got away with it and I must suffer the consequences.

The weekend was long and drawn out, with the boys at least enjoying themselves playing with the several children that lived around Mum's secluded estate. On Monday morning I kept a previously arranged appointment with the solicitor and travelled into Livingston alone. The bus route passed my home, and I felt myself tense at the prospect of Sam catching the same bus. I strained my neck to examine the figures standing by the bus stop, forcing a bitten fingernail hard into my teeth. He wasn't there.

John received me with the typical impersonal efficiency that I was now accustomed to. His windowless office always seemed in an arranged kind of chaos, with John being able to find what he was looking for without too much paper shuffling. I signed the various papers that were presented to me before telling him about the assault and the proposed move. He seemed neither surprised nor shocked at the news. He didn't ask how or why it happened, only who was involved nodding quickly when he knew that Debbie and Sonia were not any of his clients.

'So where are they sending you?' he asked, tapping a pen against his teeth in rhythmic clicks. I shook my head without answer. I felt drained and listless sitting in that office watching him stab out the refuge office's phone number. He smiled, greeting Irma almost with affection.

'Where is Susan Brown going, any idea? Hmm. Yeah, Longstone Road. Right, no problem. Aye. Okay then, speak to you later.'

'Looks like refuge two, Mrs Brown, I'll redirect your mail from here and needless to say it has nothing to do with any of your cases, so no worries there.'

Waves of nausea slowed me down as I made my way towards the next port of call, the housing offices. Two cups of coffee had been my breakfast that morning and I considered stopping to buy some chocolate to eat on the way back to Mum's.

Babies and toddlers seemed to swarm the confectionery aisle and my gaze rested on an angelic little girl dressed in pale shades of blue complete with a blue hair clip that prevented fair wisps of hair from falling onto her face. She looked about two years old, maybe three. I watched her hesitant movements as she surveyed the choice of sweets that her mother listed quietly behind her. This was the third day without Rosie and I craved her soft little hand holding mine as she looked for sweeties. I ached to hear her voice, her constant chatter. I wanted to smooth this little girl's fringe and brush her velvet cheek and smell her soap-scented hair and imagine her being Rosie with me for just that moment. 'Get used to it girl,' I thought, struggling to keep the knot in my throat from developing into an audible sob. 'This is how it'll be if he gets custody. You can do this, so get used to it.'

It was still early enough for the housing office to be deserted and quiet when it normally boasted a constant queue for attention. The reception desk was clean and clear of everything save the computer keyboard and screen behind which the clerk sat smiling her greeting in a relaxed manner. She tapped in my details on screen, apologising for the delay as she dashed away towards the office at the back of the building.

A middle-aged woman moved silently towards the row of chairs and we politely exchanged resigned smiles of patience while we waited in silence.

'Right, Mrs Brown, there has been a bit of a hold up,' she

almost whispered the statement glancing at the woman seated behind me. 'We received your application and part of the processing procedure includes the need for an up-to-date statement of your present rent or . . . what is it? . . no, it's your mortgage,' she said, examining my application form. She shifted her gaze from the application form to me. She was neatly presented, and neatly dressed in smart, well-fitted clothes. Her hair was newly cut, styled into a bob and her make-up was light and complete. I was close enough to notice her lightly mascaraed eyelashes, each hair neatly separated with fashionable black. I suddenly wondered what I looked like in comparison. 'Well, we're still waiting for your reply, Mrs Brown,' she said gently.

'I've never received any letters. That's why I'm here really. I'm now actually homeless and . . .'

'Well, we wrote to you . . . let me see, on 13 July.' I shook my head and she looked puzzled. She offered me the letter and my heart sank when I read the address.

'Oh great,' I muttered bitterly.

Despite my underlined warnings not to send any correspondence to my address, they had in fact gaily ignored the exclamation marks and addressed their enquiry just so. The woman bit into her pale pink lips, frowning down at my letter of explanation that had been stapled on top of the application form. I had asked for any letters to be sent to Mum's address. 'And now you say you are homeless?'

'Yes.'

'And you don't have the statement with you?'

'No.' My face remained expressionless and I had visions of Sam reading the letter, and promptly moving the statement from its usual place where we kept similar papers.

She apologised profusely, and I nodded resignedly. She promised to phone the building society for the statement, and I smiled politely. She detailed the procedure for house allocations and I listened intently. Once my points had been set, I'd go onto the housing list and, as a homeless person, I must accept the first house that was offered. This was regardless of its condition and location. If I refused the offer, it would be 12 months before I would be allowed to return to the list for my second try for a house.

Of course my situation was desperate, I thought irritably on my way out, wasn't everyone's? Every day the council's housing stocks were being depleted because of house sales. Every day people of all ages were joining the queue for housing. And like me, they either were homeless or would be shortly. There were hundreds of us, thousands probably, all desperately scraping and grasping, all fervently hoping for that one phone call, that one letter offering them the tenancy of a house.

When Frances called me that afternoon, my instructions were to go up to their office the following morning and they would take me back to the refuge to collect my belongings. One of the families in refuge two was willing to change places with me. 'Wasn't that nice of her?' Frances asked, as if trying to rekindle my faith in womankind.

We packed up to leave Mum's house again, this time without Rosie who would at least miss out on this enforced resettlement. No one had expressed any interest in exchanging houses with Mum, and even this week's advert wasn't going in because we couldn't afford it between us. 'Still,' she said, 'maybe this refuge will have a nice lassie living there.' There was little hope left within me about anything though.

We all kissed goodbye again and promised to phone as soon as possible. She stood at her door watching us go, her beautiful garden cheerily shouting out radiant colours and life while the day was warming up into another scorcher. We endured the bus journey into town silently wrestling with our own thoughts, until David burst into floods of tears that splashed down onto his T-shirt like ink spots. I held him gently in my attempt to comfort him, but all my efforts went into staying dry-eyed myself. It was all I could do for him. I couldn't answer his constant questions about where we were going now, and would he still be able to travel to his old school etc. If there were any decisions left for me, I doubt I would have been mentally capable of making one anyway. Everything seemed to be so out of my control.

Our reception at the office was initially calm and friendly, with Wanda ushering the boys into another room to watch television. I was introduced to Irma, whose voice on the phone matched the woman in appearance. In her late 50s, she had a genuine manner, and kindly eyes and she sat in one of only two chairs that occupied the otherwise spotless room. 'How do you feel?' she said quietly once the door was closed and we were alone. I sat perched on the chair, clutching my handbag on my knee, and was already aware of the constant ache in my shoulders. As I detected the note of sympathy in her question I answered honestly while gazing down at the carpet.

'Bloody awful, Irma. I feel betrayed, alone, let down and bloody pissed off! That's how I feel.'

'Let down by who?' She leant forward in her chair, her hands poised to light her cigarette.

'By everyone. Them at the refuge, Frances and Wanda . . .'

'*What!*' she mouthed in a forced whisper. The expression on her face was one of utter shock and our eyes locked onto each other. Then Frances came into the room.

'Susan says she feels you've let her down!' Irma blurted to Frances who immediately tutted looking mortally wounded by the suggestion.

'And why should you feel let down by us?' she demanded, crossing her arms.

'Because you don't believe me, that's why.' I was unrepentant.

'But I told you on the phone that we didn't think you were lying, Susan.'

'Aye, but you're still doing nothing about Debbie!'

'That's because we don't have any proof that she assaulted you, we told you all this.'

'And Frances had to come into work especially yesterday, just to meet the policewoman you called, even she said there was no proof,' Irma added. The cat fight escalated.

'But what about all the other stuff? Christ, what about all the other bloody rules that were broken. Isn't that enough to kick them out?' I shouted. 'Jesus, Sonia's got a bloody house to go to after all.'

'Any decisions about who goes where and when are ours to make,' Frances shot back.

'I think you should apologise for that Susan . . . Wanda, you'll never guess what?' Irma announced as Wanda squeezed herself into an overheated room, 'Susan thinks we've all let her down, and she thinks we should evict Debbie and Sonia.' Irma had it in for me.

'All right.' I lifted my hands up, trying to introduce calm into this supposed meeting. 'What did you do the last time this happened?'

'It's never happened before!'

'You're joking!' I gasped.

'Nope,' Frances confirmed smugly.

At three against one, the odds were clearly not in my favour. Nevertheless, I continued to fight my corner. Wanda explained the situation again to me, as if I'd perhaps been absent somehow but it gave me time to think. She pointed out that they'd all given their utmost to resolve this problem, and they'd spelt out every choice available to me along the way. Now, it was obvious that I was less than happy with the way things had gone, and less than appreciative too. 'You see, doing things like calling the police doesn't do the refuge any favours you know.' Wanda explained.

'So I wasn't supposed to call the police?' It was a genuine question that I wanted them to answer, but the women raised their eyes to the ceiling in exasperation.

'Look, I'm not trying to be difficult here, it's a real question. Was I not supposed to press charges?'

Wanda turned from the window. 'It was your prerogative, Frances told you that. But it certainly didn't go in anyone's favour.'

'Well, why didn't she say so when I asked her opinion?' Another wrong decision marked its place in my mental book.

'Bad reports like this could effectively close us down you know.' God, I thought, I've put the entire charity into jeopardy.

'Look, if you'd wanted it kept from the police, you only had to bloody say . . . and anyway, apart from all that, let's get back to Debbie and Sonia. What about all the other offences they've committed while receiving your hospitality and why won't you move them instead of me?'

Irma tutted irritably, shifting positions in her seat. 'We've considered all that, and it's our decision what we do and remember this, Susan, you hardly kept us informed of events while you were there as you're all supposed to do.' She jabbed a finger in my direction. 'We've been running this refuge for 11 years you know, so don't think you can walk in here and tell us what to do next,' Frances stated firmly.

'What's the point in having rules when you don't stick by them?' I was crying and shouting at this point. I felt cornered and confused, and utter frustration about their inability to see my side of things. 'Christ, I wish I'd smacked that cow back now that I know neither of us would've been kicked out.'

'Then you both would've been evicted. Look, Susan, we've given you your options, and you've decided to go to our second refuge, is this right?' Wanda asked calmly. 'You'll still have to go by the rules there too. You'll still have to report any abuses, just like everyone else does.'

'And you'll believe me?' I asked bitterly, willing her to answer, but she sighed in an exaggerated manner. Her attitude was similar to one used by a tired nursery teacher with a wilful child.

'It's your choice,' Frances repeated.

'I have no bloody choice!' I screamed at them, and they recoiled in unison. 'I have to move, don't I, there is no bloody choice!'

'Nobody's making you move, you can stay where you are if you want.' Wanda crossed her arms in matronly fashion.

'Oh aye, and have their kids kick the shit out of mine whenever they felt like it? Do you think I could put them through all that, do you think they deserve any of this?' I yelled. 'Oh, I've got choices all right. If you want to put it that way, I could choose to move back into my home with my bastard of a husband, couldn't I, and I could choose to stay there and be abused for a few more years,' I ranted.

'See, now you're just being silly!' Frances snorted.

'I have no choices,' I repeated feeling exhausted and weak. 'If you won't move them, then I have no choice.'

'I think you should apologise for what you said earlier,' Irma croaked reproachfully. 'It's just not fair to accuse us of not doing enough for you with this problem.'

I kept a constant gaze at the grey carpet, while Frances and Wanda wandered in turn from the door to the window. Then one of them stopped in front of me. 'Of course, if you feel that we're not being effective in our attempts to help, and you feel that you might like to go elsewhere . . . you're quite entitled to. There are other hostels and refuges to go to, you don't have to stay here.'

This was it. This was the ultimatum. Either shut you're mouth girl, or go somewhere else. Where? A council hostel? And where would that be?

'No,' I rasped, 'I'll just go to refuge two . . . if that's okay with you.'

'Are you sure?' Frances asked, and I glanced up to check her expression.

'It doesn't matter any more. Just move us, it doesn't matter,' I whimpered.

Thursday, 3 August 1995

They huffed and puffed and petulantly drove me back to the refuge. Debbie was in, but never looked my way once. Wanda and Frances helped me pack my things and ordered a quick meeting of inmates. Wanda read the riot act to Margaret, Debbie and me, promising all the spot-checks that they never bothered to execute during the past six weeks. Sonia had scarpered. As we were leaving, a smartly dressed woman approached the door asking to see Jean. I told her that Jean was out and was due back this afternoon. She smiled mischievously, shaking a set of keys in the air. 'Tell her it's the housing officer,' she said, shrugging her shoulders gleefully.

CHAPTER THIRTEEN

Refuge two was a smaller house, in a smaller housing estate in a smaller town. Nolleen lived there, with her two toddler boys. She was a slim girl, about 25 with dark hair and large brown eyes but she rarely looked at me. Nolleen said 'what?' to absolutely anything and everything I said to her.

'Can I use this cupboard, Nolleen?'

'What?'

'This cupboard, okay?'

'Aye, sure.'

'What day do the buckets go out?'

'What?'

'Bucket day, it's Wednesday, right?'

'Aye, Wednesday.'

'If it's okay, I'll hang out the washing.'

'What?'

After an hour of that and noting the absence of a hearing aid, I concluded that she was not very communicative and promptly gave up making small talk.

Compared to the constant din of the first refuge this one was terminal in its silence. My bedroom was bigger though, clean enough and with a set of bunk beds for the boys, a single for me and a cot for Rosie. I half-heartedly unpacked one or two of the five black bags that contained all our things, and made up the beds while the boys explored the back garden. Flashbacks of that morning's screaming match at the office plagued me, and I felt despondent and emotional. Snatches of dialogue repeated themselves over and over, with my imagination creating better lines that I could have said in the endless script.

I busied myself on that first day cleaning every possible surface of coal dust, grease, porridge, toffee, chewing gum and something white which stuck to the arms of the three-piece suite. Nolleen and the other resident Sharon (who was now being driven back to my first refuge) had obviously discarded the rota system for house chores. Nobody had cleaned anything static in the house for weeks. Half circles of handprints covered the area around the door handles.

Just like the first refuge, this house had all the furniture and white goods anyone needed within a normal household. I had imagined a cash-strapped organisation being unable to supply luxuries such as washing machines and fully carpeted rooms. Bedding was plentiful and without hint of a candlewick bedspread. The beds looked fairly modern and had new mattresses. The kitchens had second-hand electric cookers, microwaves, toasters and electric kettles with the washing machines always looking new. The plates and cutlery were odd, but overflowing in the cupboards along with other kitchen items and baking trays. The two refuge houses were plainly decorated and it was clearly up to the residents to keep them reasonably clean, if not for themselves, at least for their children.

Flies buzzed around the lightshade in the living-room with baby ones crowding the kitchen window sill. The 'phone cupboard' had a wooden ledge running round the plaster walls, which had been used as an ashtray for whoever was using the phone. At regular intervals along this ledge, cigarette stubs sat bent over like a line of drunk men. I remembered Irma telling me that she called into the refuge every Wednesday, and the state of this house's cleanliness only cemented the doubts I had about her statement.

However, once Nolleen had left saying she'd be back in the afternoon, cleaning the house gave me something to do and I opened the door and windows to encourage some air into the house.

The partly paved garden was overgrown and beige with sun-beaten grass that had turned to straw. Ryan threw himself energetically around the garden, fighting some invisible force that was attacking our defences, while David searched for grass spiders amongst the undisturbed growth.

I imagined Sharon and her son settling into the bedroom I'd cleared with Frances and Wanda that morning and remembered her red grinning face when we'd exchanged black bags at refuge two.

'It's going to be great at your bit,' she enthused, hauling three bags behind her along the front path towards the van. 'My sister lives near there, and my pals like. You're welcome to this place!' she'd jerked her head in the house's direction. 'I was over the moon when they said we could change places.'

'Aye, me too,' I'd answered flatly, glancing at Fiona, who'd merely pursed her lips at my sarcasm.

I made sandwiches for the boys' lunch and watched them eating them while I sipped a coffee. My lack of appetite was worse than ever.

'So, what do you think so far?'

'Its all right now that you've cleaned it up a bit,' David offered.

'Not much to do here,' Ryan added quietly, watching my expression.

'No, I'm not keen on it either, son, but at least there's no Jade and Jamie attacking you every five minutes, and Nolleen doesn't look like much of a raver either.'

I phoned Mum, who sounded relieved to hear me. I only hinted at the trauma I'd suffered at the refuge office and tried to sound light and happy at the prospect of being in this new safe house. I wanted her to believe that things were improving, that her Jonah daughter had at last found somewhere reasonably safe to stay, that things would now settle down and she needn't worry so much. Recent events had weighed heavily on her, with her natural reaction being one of helplessness in her need to protect her own. She was the only family member who cared, or even knew what was happening to me and the kids. Now we were even further away from her, and after our phone call I felt more desolate and alone.

When Nolleen returned carrying a single bag of shopping, I called the boys in and grabbed my purse.

'Where's the local shop, Nolleen?'

'What?'

'I need to get milk, is the shop just round the corner?'

'Aye, just up the road,' she pointed lamely in the general direction. 'Up, and round the corner. They'll take tokens,' she added. It was the most she'd said to me since we'd arrived that morning.

On the way up to the shop, we passed a battered red car parked on our side of the road. The motor gently idled and I glanced at the man in the driver's seat as we walked past him.

The boys bickered noisily with each other, stopping only to place their orders for sweets and comics which I numbly nodded agreement to. I thought so much about what had happened that I barely noticed any life around me. I couldn't stop thinking about it and automatic tasks like wandering to the shop for milk offered little distraction.

When we got back to the house, I let myself in through the front door and we trooped innocently through the hall to the living-room. Both boys were examining the front pages of their comics as they wandered into the room, and I carried on towards the kitchen with the milk that I'd just bought when I first saw him.

It was an innocent scene that greeted us. A man was calmly helping his girlfriend to empty her shopping bags. He stood in the kitchen staring at the contents of the bag he was holding, while she placed tins into a cupboard above her head. They chatted quietly together, unaware of my presence. I think if I'd been wearing boots my heart would have been firmly embedded in them at that point.

Giant-sized images of the print that was typed on the rules and regulations flashed before me. NO MEN ALLOWED INTO THE REFUGE. Refuge workers' faces flickered before me, demanding I tell them anything and everything, warning me what would happen if I didn't tell them, and here it was already. My first day and there it was, a man in a battered woman's refuge!

'Who's he, and what's he doing here?' I demanded, raising my voice enough for them to snap their heads round in unison.

'Aw . . . it's okay, he's just a pal,' Nolleen said half smiling, her eyes nervously darting between us.

'But he's just going!' I snapped, staring at him hard.

He stood limply clutching a carton of cornflakes, like a child caught in some trivial act by a teacher. I glanced back at the boys, their eyes already registering fear. 'It's okay, he's just leaving,' I shouted back to them, and he promptly nodded, bending to drop the bag gently onto the floor before squeezing past me to leave.

Nolleen continued to fill the cupboards and promptly appeared at the door muttering something about having to go somewhere. She averted her eyes from me, almost jogging towards the front door, and I felt glad she was clearing out. Both boys turned towards me. 'Mum, you're not going to tell the workers are you?' they pleaded. Their eyes were wide and frightened again and I smoothed their hair, shaking my head. 'Don't tell them 'cos they'll just move us again.'

I felt numb about the situation. I couldn't believe what fate had thrown me head first into and a thousand questions careered around my head like frantic children all talking at once. How many times had this happened before? Maybe Nolleen and Sharon did this kind of thing all the time, inviting their boyfriends in for the night even? Didn't anyone spot-check this place either? What else went on here? 'It's all right, don't worry, I won't say a word, I won't tell them.' I soothed. Christ, they'd never believe me anyway.

Thursday, 3 August (contd)
She came back about 9.30 p.m. with her boys and quietly put them to bed. When she came into the living-room I told her straight that I wanted to go by the rules, no men, no booze, no parties. She dumbly agreed (she didn't say 'What?') and I went to bed. I lay awake listening to the boys' breathing and ached for Rosie's warm wee body to be beside me, jabbing me with her knees and elbows. I listened for Nolleen answering the door to her boyfriend, imagining her whispering, 'It's okay, she's gone to bed'. But she turned in herself about an hour after me.

The night passed without incident, and I spent the majority of it thinking, and planning a day out for the boys. I need money though, and the town we're in is so small, it doesn't have a cash machine. That means travelling into Edinburgh hoping that the DSS has paid my money as promised. If not, how would we get back? This is the constant pattern of my life these days. Every task is peppered with additional worry and salted with the constant threat of failure.

Telling the workers about the boyfriend in the house was never an option I considered. Again it would be my word against theirs and another unbelievable accusation could mean a swift eviction. What worried me though, was their finding out by themselves and the tearfully muttered promise I'd made to squeal about any further abuses echoed back to me. The following day was Wednesday, Irma's day for visiting the refuge.

David and Ryan nodded enthusiastically at my suggestion for a day out in Edinburgh and obediently padded downstairs to wash and brush their teeth without my having to ask twice.

Nolleen was up with her two tots, who stood beside her in the kitchen staring up at me in complete silence. They were miniatures of Nolleen, right down to the small dark eyes and short black hair. They both looked around two or three years of age but they were not twins.

I did not attempt to make conversation with any of them and set about getting breakfast for my lot while she loaded the washing machine. We stepped around each other in a bizarre ballet, making movements precise enough never to make physical contact even once. 'We're going out for the day,' I said as she passed on her way into the kitchen. We were fed and watered, washed and dressed, ready to leave.

'What?'

'We're going in-to Edin-bur-gh!' I repeated, shouting from the living-room.

David and Ryan seemed genuinely excited about their day out and a promised trip to the cinema. They chattered constantly, discussing the merits of each film I'd read from the local free paper I'd found at the refuge. Anyone passing us in the street would see a woman with two boys chatting brightly beside her as they walked towards their day out.

I cried all the way through the film and tears meandered down my face and dripped off my jaw onto my T-shirt. I wiped my eyes with my sleeves when the blurred images became too distorted. I could weep quietly, allowing my face to contort itself into the undignified shape everyone's face does when they are crying. The film had captured the boy's attention enough for them to stop glancing up at me to see if I was laughing. To them, it was obvious that I was enjoying the film. I was even shaking and trembling with silent laughter it was so funny. The darkness allowed me that for nearly two hours and if the boy's noticed that I had been crying they never said.

Afterwards, we went for a walk, stopping to look inside any shops that interested the boys. We looked so ordinary, behaved so ordinarily the three of us. We didn't look anxious and unsettled like homeless people do. We didn't look desperate. Desperate for money, desperate for housing, desperate for a break. We didn't look as if we would jump the height of ourselves if a loud car horn blasted out beside us in a way that people who endure unpredictable acts of violence against them do. The boys neither cowered nor shrunk back at other people's actions and they could laugh, talk and play along with the rest of the world's children. There was no sign on my forehead saying 'HELP!' and no one stopped me and said, 'Good God girl, are you all right?'

We bought chips, three bags, and wandered into Princes Street Gardens. People knelt, crouched, sat and lay on the grass, soaking up the sun enjoying the warmth, and we picked a reasonably clean patch of grass on which to sit and eat our lunch. I tried to eat, but the tart smelling chips which had been doused with vinegar almost made me retch and I dumped the bag down onto the grass beside me and started to cry again. Every thought I had was an attempt to solve one of my problems. But they overwhelmed me. Once I had raked over one worry, another one would smartly jump in its place. They all crowded round me for attention, pulling at my clothes and jostling for position. What about the boys? How would they cope with another new school? What about Rosie? How could any of us cope with only seeing her one weekend out of two if Sam gained custody? How would she react? If Nolleen insisted on breaking the refuge rules, what then? How long would we have to stay there before we were offered a house? Months, a year maybe?

I snorted, and sniffed and bubbled uncontrollably while the boys sullenly ate their lunch beside me. David wiped a salty hand on his shorts before placing it gently across my shoulders saying, 'It's okay, Mum, it's okay,' to my constant apologies. They depended on me for everything and I was responsible for the sorry state we were in. It had been my decision to leave the family home to enter a refuge. It was my decision to confront Debbie that night when Sonia had left her children and the consequences of that meant our having to be moved elsewhere. My decision to stay quiet about the latest incident could just as easily worsen our situation further. The effect of these episodes was magnified by the fact that Sam was so obviously getting away with it; no individual, no court would ever confront him with the way he'd treated his family.

In fact, the courts would not only allow him to stay in the house while the children and I remained homeless, but they could also give him full custody of our daughter. The possibility of this weighed more heavily on my mind than anything else.

The least I could do now was to acknowledge every appalling mistake I'd made since the day we'd left home and apologise. They knew exactly why their Mum was crying over their lunchtime picnic on that otherwise beautiful sunny day. They didn't have to be told and they didn't ask. They just knew. 'Anyway,' I spluttered into a crumpled tissue, 'I've got an idea. I'll phone Dad and see if he can help.'

'What, Grandad?' Ryan asked, peering into my blotched face for confirmation.

We squeezed into the shaded telephone box and I squinted at the minute number printed on the address pages of my diary. Not only had I not seen my dad for over four years at that point, I'd had no reason to phone him for an innocent chat either. As far as he knew, I was married for the second time and living happily in West Lothian with my husband and three healthy children in a house with a bidet. He gained all his information from Malcolm and would remember the bit about the bidet. It would appeal to his sense of achievement. Even Malcolm, who held a highly paid managerial post with a national sales firm, didn't have a bidet.

'Hello? Is Donald there?' It was Robert, one of Dad's business partners.

'Er . . . no, he's not. I think he's at the other shop.'

'Right, then, can I get the number . . . it's Susan, his daughter, here.'

'Emm . . . well, I don't know really.' There was an agonising wait while this man I'd never met in my life considered the request, obviously wondering if I was genuinely Donald's daughter. 'Look,' he said at last, 'he's due here in a couple of hours. I'll tell him you called, he can phone you back.'

'I'm in a phone box, Robert, I can't hang around for another two bloody hours . . . oh, never mind!' I snapped and jammed the receiver down into it's cradle. If I could have spoken to Dad, and somehow explained my unbelievable situation, he might have been able to offer me some sort of hope. If he could cover the deposit on a rented house somewhere we could move out of the refuge system altogether.

It was a long shot, but the £300 to £400 that was needed could only come from him since nobody else I knew had that kind of money. But he wasn't available, and the brightest idea I'd had that day faded quietly away. Now I was visibly clutching at straws and I pushed some more silver into the phonebox and punched out Mum's number.

'Hi Mum.'

'Where are you hen?' she'd already noted the emotional tone of my voice.

'In Edinburgh, we've been to the pictures . . . Mum, are there any calls about an exchange?' I was desperate for her to say yes. For her to be excited and full of news, good news about the future.

'Nope,' she said crisply.

'I . . . I tried to phone Dad today, Mum.' My voice began to crack. 'I thought that maybe he could help us . . . you know, with the money for a deposit on a rented house . . . but he wasn't even in!' I sobbed. My head ached with the pain of trying not to cry. My throat felt dry and burnt with the effort of keeping tears at bay and waves of complete helplessness seemed to swamp me, as we all stood inside that telephone box.

'It's okay, I did get a call about an exchange. I just didn't want to tell you in case it built your hopes up,' she said between squeaks and croaks from my end of the line. 'There's this man, sounds really keen. I've been to see the district, it's lovely, just right for us.'

'Oh good,' I whimpered, trusting her every word. 'I just thought that Dad could help, I'm so bloody desperate Mum, I don't want to go back and I've been racking my brains trying to find a way out . . .'

'Well, come here then, just for a visit,' she urged. I hesitated, wanting to go straight to her door as usual, but various reasons for not going danced around my mind confusing me further.

'Does this guy sound keen to exchange then?' I wanted to hear more, to be assured that things could improve, however slowly.

'Yes, he's keen . . . look, just jump on a bus, I can tell you when I see you.'

'I can't stop crying you know, and that stupid cow Nolleen had a guy in the refuge yesterday . . . can you believe it?'

'Tell me when you get here,' she said firmly.

I looked at the boys' faces, knowing they would love to go back to Nana's house where some comfort for us remained. 'We'll just be visiting this time,' I informed David and Ryan sternly and they nodded with a grin, both clasping my hands tightly.

CHAPTER FOURTEEN

While we sat on a bench, like three gnomes at Haymarket Station, Dad was careering about Waverley Station at the other end of Princes Street. Mum had managed to contact him at the other shop and had hurriedly explained the situation to him. 'I need you to go to Waverley to make sure she gets on that Bathgate train,' she'd instructed.

So he'd dropped everything and driven into town to examine the ever-changing throng of travellers that arrived every day. In his mind he had a picture of me as I had looked four years before. The boys were still only about four years of age, and of course would still look similar enough to be taken for twins. However, when he'd found the Bathgate train he'd entertained the passengers as they had watched him dart from train to platform in his bid to find his daughter and grandsons.

When the train left, he phoned Mum back to explain the failed mission. 'Christ, Kath, it was a wonder I wasn't lifted for accosting young women and looking into their faces!' he shouted above the noise of the station. 'She's not here . . . well, there wasn't anyone like her with bairns like ours,' he'd complained.

When we did arrive at Mum's her relief was obvious and she prepared to phone back all the people she had involved in her bid to get me back to West Lothian. Dad spoke to me briefly, his voice reminding me once more of damp Sunday outings and chocolate pears from that shop in Portobello High Street. 'Don't leave things so long this time,' he said. 'If you think I could help just call me, really.' We promised to keep in touch this time and he was gone.

The boys went out to play and I sat limp and exhausted on the

149

couch, pleased to be in familiar surroundings again. We briefly discussed my options once more, this time brightened by the recent note of interest placed in an exchange with Mr Murray.

There was a definite lack of space at Mum's house. Her cottage had been built for a maximum of two and boasted one single bedroom and a windowless boxroom. When we'd stayed the odd weekend with her, Mum had slept in one of the boys' bunk beds which were placed side by side in her bedroom for quickness. David and Ryan slept in either the bed or on cushions on the floor and this was decided by a rota system. I slept on Mum's bed, which had been manoeuvred into the boxroom leaving just enough space to stand up to get dressed. Once the light had been switched out, however, it was like the Black Hole of Calcutta and just as airless.

Such a claustrophobic existence would also cause us stress with a potential for chaos that could have us tearing each other's hair out before long. 'But it wouldn't be for long,' Mum said encouragingly. 'Even if Mr Brophy doesn't exchange with us, then someone else surely will and Sam won't realise that you're actually staying here, will he?'

Two years before, when Mum had first moved into her beautiful cottage, I had been pregnant with Rosie and I had felt comforted that she was only two streets away from our own home. Now her location presented itself as just another problem because Sam was so nearby. He relied on the bus service too and even the bus route passed his door. If he were to find out that I lived in such overcrowded conditions he would surely pounce on the opportunity to steal Rosie from us. Not only did he have the space but he had her very own bedroom with familiar toys awaiting her permanent return. Something I wouldn't be able to offer her for a long time.

Saturday, 5 August 1995
So, here I am at Mum's again. Another failed marriage behind me, dependent on the council for housing yet again – on Income Support – no job, three young kids and one crazy embittered bastard of an estranged husband after me as well.

Rosie came back on Friday evening, bang on time. I stood in the kitchen, avoiding the very sight of him. It seemed an age before Sam left and I could hear her excited chatter in the hallway. She squealed with delight and ran up to me and cuddled me so hard. It was bliss! I thought she'd be angry or aloof with me for abandoning her, but she was pleased to be back. She settled straight down to playing with 'her boys' as she calls them. I decided not to go back to the refuge. The boys were dreading it and we could stay at Mum's for the time it'll take the exchange to go through. Mum thinks she has someone interested. Fingers crossed . . .

I phoned the refuge office to tell them about my decision to leave and spoke to Isla, the worker who had helped us escape that first morning.

'As long as you're sure that's what you want,' she said gently. 'And you think you'll be safe enough . . . you know, with your husband living nearby.'

I gave my assurances, and she thanked me for the note I'd sent them on that first afternoon at refuge two.

I stood by my opinion about the conduct of the workers and their unfair decision about the incident with Debbie. Their running of the refuge during my time there had presented the opportunity for abuse and they'd hardly been open to criticism. Their impression was that they were far too experienced to be told how to improve their service by a mere 'resident'. Finally, their 'suggestion' that I could always move onto another organisation's hostel was both cruel and humiliating for me.

However, they had been there when I'd needed them and for that I remained truly grateful. My need for fairness meant that I should write a note apologising for my ungrateful attitude towards them that awful morning of the argument. It was short and sweet and included how low I'd felt, as if they had needed reminding.

The biggest worry about staying at Mum's was my husband's delighted discovery of the fact and his bid for custody of Rosie. As things stood, his chance of winning the case was paper thin. He had now openly rejected the step-children that were accepted into the marriage and requested no access to them whatsoever. This hardly presented him as a responsible parent. After two years of being part of a large family, Rosie would be raised as an only child with her father and separated from her brothers. The courts preferred to keep such family units together.

He had made no offer to leave the family home so that the children at least could be saved from the unfamiliar surroundings of a woman's refuge. Like me he was unemployed and, unlike me, he would need to pay a childminder to look after Rosie when he did gain suitable employment, unless of course he moved up to Stirlingshire to live with Marjery. He had no evidence to back up any claim he could make about my being an unfit mother and no witness either. I was well aware that he would be desperate to find a way of showing that I was not a good wife and mother for our children.

Not only was I the main carer for the children throughout our relationship, but I was a registered childminder as well. Everyone I knew questioned his motives for going for custody, but not me. I understood his desperate need for revenge because my need was stronger.

But things progressed so slowly. After nearly six weeks I hadn't even been granted legal aid. Even when I did, the case would have to be frozen to wait for Sam's legal assistance to be granted. It was obviously going to be months before we got to court and so Mum and I felt we could risk living in such overcrowded conditions on the quiet. It would mean walking the boys over two dual carriageways and a football field in order to get them to school and back each day. This was because the normal route would have involved them passing the door of our former home and alerting Sam to our new address.

David and Ryan immediately cheered when we told them that I had decided to leave the refuge system altogether, but we had to warn them about playing within the cul-de-sac in an attempt at keeping them away from Sam and anyone else who might know them. There could always be an observant ex-neighbour who might innocently mention it to Sam in the passing. Although Rosie's speech was clear and her comprehension matched her age, Mum and I doubted that she would actually be able to tell her Daddy that she now lived with Nana. Just in case though, we decided to refer to Nana's house as 'the refuge' and we hoped that she'd use this name should she be grilled one day by Sam.

Other problems included the restricted living space we would all have to cope with and the Housing Department's reaction to my new living conditions. I was assured that I was still considered homeless, however, they still couldn't advise me about anything until my points had been allotted. I would have to accept the first offer of housing regardless of district or condition. If I refused, I'd have to wait 12 months before being accepted back onto the waiting list once more.

Then the housing clerk suggested, almost as an afterthought, that Mum should put her name onto the transfer list. Tenants on such a privileged list are offered three houses before their application is suspended for 12 months. She shrugged her shoulders, however, when asked about an approximate waiting time for a transfer and we smiled resignedly and thanked Immaculate Clerk for her time.

This left us only with the hope of an exchange and we lived for the ring of the telephone. We had neatly handwritten cards displayed in all the local newsagents and a weekly advert inserted in the local free paper. On offer was a pensioner's cottage with one and a half bedrooms with mature gardens front and back, in a quiet district with nice elderly neighbours in exchange for a three- or four-bedroomed house in a pleasant district.

Mr Murray was the man who had noted his interest in an exchange the day I had fallen to bits in Edinburgh. He lived alone in a modern three-bedroomed bungalow at the other side of town. A widower with his family grown up and living elsewhere, he felt the house too big to maintain and was eager to settle into a pensioner's house before he retired. He kindly drove us to view his home, offering to leave beds and the odd piece of old furniture since he appreciated there wouldn't be enough room for it all in a smaller house. He seemed keen to apply for the exchange papers from the council and wanted to move with as little delay as possible.

His house was perfect for us and was situated within a quiet estate flanked by owner occupiers with neat gardens. Mr Murray's genuine enthusiasm encouraged us to think that our dream had come true at last. We started to imagine ourselves actually living there, hoping that the power of positive thought would help us towards our goal.

After a week or so, he called to tell us that he'd collected the appropriate forms for the council and that he'd soon be up to fill them in with Mum and sign them.

He admitted, however, that his daughter sometimes came home to stay with him for the odd weekend and he wondered if there would be enough room for her. Could he bring her up for a look around?

Again he expressed relief at finding such a perfect little house and his daughter appeared impressed by the room sizes and, of course, the quiet district. He'd forgotten the papers for signing, however, but he'd bring them up later that week. Another week passed by and we began to sink into dark thoughts of doubt about Mr Murray's intentions. Eventually Mum telephoned him for a definite decision. He'd changed his mind, the exchange was off and we were firmly dumped onto our backsides once more.

Such disappointments were hard to bounce back from and Mum and I found ourselves gazing enviously at houses on other estates along the bus routes we travelled. Sometimes we'd spot the black windows that signalled an empty property but this was a rare event and sometimes meant the house was for sale rather than for rent. Like most towns, ours has its rough streets and undesirable neighbourhoods. However, even empty houses in these areas could still be let to someone desperate enough, because of the lack of choice for prospective tenants. The 'Right to Buy' policy was biting hard into the housing stocks and Mum and I despaired about getting a house in a reasonable area.

Past events meant that we had lived in some of the worst council housing estates in Edinburgh. Craigentinny during my childhood had been a cold, concreted mass of unruly street-playing children traipsing through neighbours' back greens without a backward glance. We still wondered how we'd survived the year we'd spent living in West Pilton when stones had battered off our window on a nightly basis. Wester Hailes was an improvement, if only because of the lack of mouthy teenagers who crowded the door demanding a light for their cigarettes, but towards the end the Fire Brigade were never away from the drying rooms and empty flats that had been set alight by bored youths and brainless tenants. Life in such neighbourhoods was stressful, not least because of the worry that your house could be broken into and wrecked beyond recognition while you were nipping down to the shop for a pint of milk. Mum and I couldn't cope with another bad district and the effect on the boys could mean more chaos within their lives.

One day Mum and I took the kids out and Jean got on the bus at the refuge stop. I bumped myself down beside her and she seemed pleased to see me again. She talked excitedly about her new house and looked forward to moving in once the cooker, fridge and beds had been bought. I told her that I'd left refuge number two and was now staying with Mum and of our hopes of getting an exchange.

'Did you hear about Debbie?' she asked, lowering her voice. 'The workers came in less than a week after you left saying that her husband had turned up.' She nodded wisely before glancing around the bus. 'Told her to pack up her things and moved her to Stirling. Said her man had found out where she was but nobody believes that. And Sonia, she's left. She moved into her new house, and Margaret moved back in with her man. He's much better apparently.' She raised her eyes to the heavens and I nodded dumbly, not wanting to interrupt this rich vein of information that just oozed from her.

'And Sharon, you know, the lassie that changed places with you?'

'Aye?'

'She arrived, with all her black bags and stuff and she goes over to the window in the living-room and waves to someone outside. So Wanda goes over to see who she's waving at, and here it's her sister and brother-in-law sitting in a car outside the refuge waiting to take her somewhere.' We'd stepped off the bus by this time and I remained enthralled. 'So Wanda turns round and tells her to pick up her stuff and evicts her there and then for telling an outsider where the refuge was! So it's rare and quiet now, just me and Linda and I'll be out of it soon,' she chirped.

Monday, 7 August 1995
So if nothing I've bucked up their ideas about the carry on behind their backs. I remember telling Irma that I'd write a story about my case for future reference but she'd said she didn't think any of them needed a social lesson. Well, they must have learnt something.

It felt so good hearing about Debbie's enforced move. The hassle she must've had in moving all her things. The disappointment she'll feel about not getting rehoused near her pal Sonia and the worry she'll have about whether her new boyfriend can be bothered travelling all the way up there to see her every weekend. She'll know exactly why she's been moved, and so will her kids.

The children settled quickly into life at their Nana's and played long and hard with the other children on the estate. There had been no toddlers living near our last home and so Rosie only played by herself or with her brothers. Now there were several five- and six-year-old girls to entertain her endlessly and they wandered about in packs of six setting up make-believe houses and shop games. Soon her name was added to the list of children that had to be called in for lunch and dinner and, like her brothers, she bolted down her food before dashing out to play with her new-found pals. After a fortnight, a knock on the front door from a prospective playmate would see her sighing heartily before instructing David and Ryan to 'tell them I'll be out in five minutes'.

The boys became tanned and healthy looking, their mouse brown hair now bleached blond by the terrific summer we were missing. Neither Mum nor I could allow the kids to play away for longer than 20 minutes or so without our having to go out to check on their whereabouts. We seemed to be the only parents who did this, but then our recent past had made us especially nervous about the kids playing unattended outside.

Without the kids to distract me, I found myself wallowing in constant thoughts about my situation. I dipped into phases of deliberation so intense that I couldn't even register when someone had spoken to me. My diet now consisted entirely of sweetened coffee while Mum tried to encourage me to eat. This lowered my energy levels but I continued to do automatic tasks like washing-up or weeding the garden in the hope that it might occupy me.

I found it diffcult to get to sleep and I'd lie awake creating images of revenge when I would confront Sam and watch him flinch and cower at my vicious taunts of rage and frustration. Then I'd try to calm myself by focusing on something pleasant. But then Marjery's fat face would appear before me and I'd launch into a tirade of abuse about her abandonment of David and Ryan. There was so much to think about, so much that remained unresolved and so many people to be angry with. When sleep did find me, I discovered that I ground my teeth so hard that I woke up long before Rosie did with aching jaws and a dull headache. Even when Rosie was at her Dad's my eyes would snap open at 5 a.m. and my brain would begin its cycle of continuous thought.

On the run-up to one of these weekends I noticed myself

becoming highly anxious as the time neared for Sam to make his ambling appearance. The boys' reaction was to escape the scene as the thought of Sam being as close as the front door unnerved them visibly, especially Ryan.

Sometimes I'd ask Mum to hand Rosie over to him, complete with her bag of clothes, but I desperately wanted to do it myself. One time I thought I felt emotionally strong enough to be present when he brought her back after a weekend. During the last ten minutes before they appeared I felt so much distress and agitation I felt physically ill. He never spoke to Mum nor I on such occasions, and totally ignored us if we spoke or asked him a question. He couldn't even make eye contact with us, preferring to look only at Rosie.

One day he duly arrived by taxi to deliver a tearful Rosie from a residential weekend. He carried with him a half-filled black bag and held it out for me to take when he eventually reached the door. I pasted a permanent smile onto my face every time I met him, in my effort to disguise my true feelings, and I lifted my arm to accept the bag. Inside I felt good that he'd actually bothered to put some of my things together and bring them to me and I thought it signalled some sort of acceptance of the situation. Maybe he could act in a civilised manner after all. However, before I managed to even touch the bag he let it drop smartly in front of us both, my gaze watching it fall noisily to the concrete floor, his gaze still on Rosie as she scampered into the hall.

Whatever was inside was glass and had smashed, and he'd turned to walk back to his waiting taxi. Even the back of his balding head smiled smugly at this neat little trick he'd devised. 'Oh, very clever!' I said feigning surprise, 'took you all weekend to think up that one, didn't it, Sam?' He continued walking and I thumped into the living-room with the black bag and promptly burst into tears. He had hurt me again, and I felt powerless in my quest to match him. It was the simplicity of his actions that amazed me. The 'drip, drip' effect psychologists would say, and he worked it to perfection with me.

I sat in the living-room and bubbled uncontrollably while Mum tried to extract the reason for my tantrum-like reaction to Sam's latest. 'God, is that all?' she said when I'd managed to blurt it out. 'Well, you should've said "thanks" and beamed a grin at him as if nothing had happened,' she instructed.

'But he's still hurting me, and I don't know how to cope with it,' I whined.

'Hurting? Susan, he's hurting.'

'Aye, sure.'

She frowned at my instant rejection of her theory.

'He must be hurting. He's gone from being a man with a great job, a beautiful wife and young family, a lovely house complete with company car to a lonely sad waster with no prospects, no transport, not a soul to talk to from one fortnight to the next and the threat of losing his house hanging over him.' She issued a handful of tissues to Rosie who duly dumped them in my lap. Then she struggled to get up onto my knee, complaining bitterly about the effort it took. 'He's sitting alone in that great big bloody house desperate for the knock on the door that'll be you asking to come back, that's what his life involves right now!' She began to shout over Rosie's fatigued wailing and the sniffs and sobs that escaped my throat.

'Well, it's not enough!' I roared back. 'I want to hurt him more!'

'Aye, and give him another reason for taking Rosie from you,' she sighed and I knew she was right.

My freedom didn't stretch to being able to exact revenge on him without it coming back to me in the form of evidence that proved an unstable and violent personality. As much as I'd craved to belt him around the head with a baseball bat, or break into my own home and wreck the place, the consequences were too important to chance. He still had control.

The bag contained two framed cross-stitched pictures that Mum had made for me; the glass had shattered into a thousand splinters. Included was one of David's books, a toy of Ryan's and an opened letter addressed to us both about David's next hospital check-up. Some photographs of David and Ryan, and one of us all at an adventure funpark we'd visited before the baby had been born. There were no photographs of Rosie. 'He's made sure he's kept them all. You're wasting your time looking for revenge, you'd be better just letting him have his petty little victories,' Mum said.

I nodded mutely. I was well aware of the waste of time and energy vengeful thoughts were. I knew it was a hopeless, soul-destroying pastime that brightly spelt the word 'frustration' out in capital letters. I still wanted it though.

Sunday, 13 August 1995

I went to the doctor yesterday and tried not to blub while telling her the amazing tales of the past three months. I failed miserably and she seemed shocked and totally sympathetic towards my plight. She diagnosed me as clinically depressed, suggesting I try some anti-depressants to lift the terrific emotional stress I'm under. I explained the churning stomach, the agitated restlessness, the insomnia, my loss of weight, my feelings of guilt about the children and my downright hopelessness etc while she patted my knee, gently offering tissues from a box. 'And how do you feel about your husband?' she asked innocently.

'I want to kill him!' I snapped, watching her recoil at my ferocity. We settled on some counselling which she said she'd set up immediately, and I promised I'd start the short course of Prozac she prescribed. They're not addictive apparently, and if they can help me put these problems into their respective boxes then I'll take the bloody things.

On Tuesday of last week I decided to go up to the house while Sam was at training. The contents of the black bag that he'd dropped in front of me had reminded me about some important papers I still needed, and things like my passport and driving licence. I wanted to look around my house once more and maybe to take some plants from the garden to save them from certain death thanks to Sam's lack of attention. I waited at the school gates, from where I could see the bus stop that he waits at. Sure enough, two hazy figures got onto the bus, one was tall and wide just like Sam so I presumed that was him and walked smartly towards the house.

Just as I passed the first house, there was Sam at the kitchen window, examining a plant on the sill. We connected momentarily before I neatly turned about and walked calmly back the way I'd come. When I knew I was out of his sight, I ran as fast as I could back over the field. I could not believe it. The one day I decide to visit the house after five long weeks, and it's his day off!

I returned the following Thursday, and this time Sam was out. However, he'd changed the locks on the door and I stood furious and disappointed on the doorstep. Dark memories of my being locked out by him during our marriage returned to me then, with me tapping pathetically on the glass outer door hoping the children were still sleeping.

I showed remarkable restraint in not alerting him to the fact that I knew about the door locks and discussed the problem with Mum when Rosie's next weekend arrived. Mum volunteered to phone him to say that we'd both bring Rosie up for her access visit and that I'd be looking out some personal items.

'I have some items packed already for her,' he replied. 'You may come to collect them.'

'She's entitled to enter her own home, Sam.'

'There's no point, it's all packed and ready. There's no need for her to come,' he said, and promptly hung up.

He wasn't about to let me past the doorstep, and I was determined to prove him wrong. I wanted inside that house even if it was the last thing I ever did. I phoned the police station and explained the situation to the control room officer. He seemed to understand immediately and suggested without hesitation that two officers accompany me in my quest to retrieve some of my belongings. We arranged a time and a meeting place and hurriedly explained things to May who had volunteered to look after Ryan and David. Then Mum and I prepared Rosie for her stay at her Daddy's and headed off towards the dual carriageway.

We would have travelled in complete silence but for Rosie's excited chatter and an impending sense of doom that engulfed me as I pushed the buggy as fast as possible through the roughly grassed playing fields. My mouth was dry and my stomach fired up its familiar signal of nerves. I was desperate to get there, imagining Sam's face at the sight of two policemen on the scene. The police car appeared at the rendezvous on cue and I pointed out the house to the officers.

CHAPTER FIFTEEN

Once the policemen had stepped from their car and sized up the house, one of them informed me that should Sam refuse them entry, by law they'd be obliged to stay on the doorstep.

'But I could break my way in?' I glanced at the windows, already imagining myself raiding the garage for a hammer to break through one of the panels on the glass door.

'You're entitled to force your way in but we wouldn't be able to assist you in any way,' the fair-haired officer warned.

At that point Sam approached the door, his face looking pale and strained. Rosie struggled from her buggy and I left Mum and the policemen and walked smartly towards him. My heart pounded like some monotonous drum and I constantly warned myself to keep calm. After lifting Rosie from her buggy she happily stepped inside and ran towards the living-room.

I looked up at Sam, averting his eyes as usual, and calmly stepped inside the vestibule to stand beside him.

'Come in, gents,' I said to the officers behind me and I noticed their combined gaze at Sam's immense height, which was worsened by the elevated vestibule. I looked childlike in comparison as we stood together for that last time ever.

'Good evening, sir,' they chorused, moving forward together.

'Just stay where you are,' Sam stated.

'Now sir, your wife is only wishing to collect some items from her home and we don't want any bother now, do we?'

'There will be no bother,' Sam returned.

'Then you won't mind us coming in then?'

'Yes, I do.' He was standing his ground and I looked at him, incredulous at his determined stance. He was wearing a rare summer outfit I noted. He had jeans that were cut off at the knee allowing me to see his tree-trunk legs which were trembling, shaking visibly. Before then I had imagined such descriptions belonged to fictional books and comic strips.

'As owner of this house I forbid you entrance,' he said majestically, crossing his ample arms across his chest. The officers remained on the doorstep.

'As owner of this house I request you enter!' I snapped back looking up at Sam. I mentally reminded myself to maintain the air of calm and civility. Visions of my being able to brush my giant, brutish husband aside remained just that, a useless vision of hope.

While the three men bickered beside me, I glanced up the hall at Rosie standing patiently at the living-room door.

Everything about my beautiful house returned to me then. The amount of light that spilled from the patio doors into the living-room and the colours of the expensive wallpaper and deep, deep carpets. Even the slight whiff of dampness that hung in the air around the concreted vestibule permeated my thoughts and I walked into the hall and past the four black bags that Sam had lined up for me.

The living-room was still warm from the heat of the day despite one of the patio doors being slightly open. It seemed barn-like compared to Mum's poky rooms cluttered with children and furniture. Sam had re-arranged the photographs, making sure that only ones of Rosie adorned the walls.

'Look Mummy!' She pointed a finger towards the evening sun. 'See garden!' She tried to catch my attention but I didn't answer. Seizing my chance I dived towards the plastic set of drawers inside the wall cabinet which was where we kept important papers. Sam suddenly appeared behind me, so close in fact that one of his shins pressed against by back as I crouched in front of the wall unit.

'What do you want?' he demanded irritably.

Before he'd finished we were both startled by the enormous boom of the living-room door closing, forced by the wind that rushed through and out of the still open front door.

On hearing this, both officers dived into the hallway opening the living-room door with grim expressions and gasping breath.

'It's okay,' Sam raised his hands but remained standing behind me. 'It's only because the front door is open.' His voice cracked slightly at the policmen's reaction, but I carried on sifting through several drawers. Sam's attention was drawn towards the officers now standing in his living-room.

'You can leave again.'

'Well, we're here now, sir' one of them shrugged. 'Your wife would have to agree to us leaving,' he smiled.

I stacked up my passport and driving licence on the unit, and thought about looking for the mortgage statement that I needed for the housing department.

'What are you looking for?' he boomed at me while they all looked on. I opened the cupboard and grabbed at a pile of glossy photographs that leaned neatly against the wall. Further back I spied the only photograph that exists of me as a baby, an A5 black and white image of me at 18 months. I had forgotten about it and felt glad that I'd retrieved it.

'What do you want, tell me what you're looking for and I'll get it for you!' His voice was demanding and strained.

If the officers had not been there I am certain that Sam would have been screaming maniacally at this point. His kingdom had been breached and his frustration glowed in his face. I stood up to scan the shelves, looking at letters that might have been addressed to me. Everytime I touched something of his he roared into my ear beside me like a five-year-old. 'That's mine! . . . Mine, leave it! . . . that's mine too!' The officers looked on mutely.

My shadow and I moved towards the door and I ran up the stairs three at a time, while Sam thumped behind me trying to keep up. I charged into Rosie's bedroom and swung open the wardrobe doors to dive into an Ottoman there. 'What are you looking for? . . . What are you looking for? . . . Hello, hello!' he repeated sarcastically and I revelled at his distress. I wanted to answer him, but I managed to stay silent.

My powers of concentration were completely shot at this point and he was standing so close I could feel the heat from his body. His breathing was laboured and on glancing up at him his face was coursed with sweat running in rivulets from his temples.

'Look at the mess!' he squealed as one of the officers joined us in the bedroom.

The bedroom looked extremely tidy and I haphazardly pulled out reams of dog-eared papers and folders, most of which I didn't even recognise let alone need to examine. His overbearing presence distracted me beyond belief and I would have given up and walked out but for the obvious anxiety I was causing him.

I spotted Rosie's toys, neatly enclosed inside one of the boys' blue toy boxes.

'NO!' he boomed, watching me pick up the pedal car Rosie had received for her first birthday.

'I have no toys for Rosie!' I snapped back, attempting to walk towards the stairs with it.

'Well, tough!' He made a grab for it.

'Don't you want your daughter to have any toys, Sam?' I asked before dark policeman intervened.

'Personal items, wasn't it?' he asked me quietly.

'Aye, this is Rosie's car,' he spat and I felt the sharp pang of his satisfaction at the officer's decision.

I dropped the car where I stood and moved quickly towards the stair, forcing Sam and the officer to trail behind me. I scanned the bookcase on the landing.

'That's mine, officer, that's my book she's got!' he whined, feeling encouraged by his last decision. I dropped the book instantly and moved downstairs.

'You've changed the locks on the door.' In the hall we three squeezed together.

'Yes, well, I'm entitled to.' His breathing was becoming laboured.

'Where's my set of keys?'

'That's right, sir,' dark policeman stated coolly, 'you must supply her with a set.'

'I'll just take them now.' I glanced past them towards the door as if willing to take the set dangling from the lock.

'No! I don't have another set . . . I'll get another made,' he said.

'And make sure you do!' I jabbed a finger in the air before charging through to the kitchen, still clutching my photographs against my chest.

I opened drawers, staring blankly into them, desperately hoping to see something of mine that I could justify taking, but Sam was beside me once more, breathing into my face, forcing his fat belly against my arms as I moved around the kitchen. Both policemen waited in the hall, leaning against the stair banister chatting to Mum who had joined them. Meanwhile, Sam and I shuffled about together in the farcical situation and I wondered how we must have looked at that point.

We were very much alone in the kitchen with no one paying attention to our dance and I decided the opportunity was too ripe to ignore. I turned around to follow him about. I raised my eyes to his reddened face and shuffled up close to him, his sweat seeping through my T-shirt as I gently pushed so that I was walking forwards and he was treading back.

All the while I looked into his face, willing him to look back, and eventually it clicked for him. He realised what I was doing and we both stopped moving. I stared into his eyes, my mouth smiling slightly but my eyes remaining bright and menacing. I wanted him to know I was no longer scared. That I could get this close to him without crumbling into nervous hysterics. That I too could be as outwardly controlled as he wished to appear. That I was not only his equal, I was his worst fear. I could do what he would never contemplate. I was his superior.

We connected in utter silence. Sweat meandered down his nose and chin and he looked grey, worn and tired. For that second or two I smiled at my tormentor before he turned away from me and looked towards the door. 'Officer!' he whinged pathetically, 'she's pushing me!'

Outside, we shoved the black bags into the footwells of the tiny police car, appreciating the offer of a lift down the road from the officers. They seemed relieved to be out of it, whereas I felt truly elated. Mum and I giggled excitedly, the harrowing experience now behind us and I imitated Sam's last pitiful sentence as if uttered by a put-upon toddler.

'He seemed such a reasonable guy,' they said in tones of amazement, nodding with each other in agreement.

'Yeah, well, that "reasonable guy" has lived there, refusing me entry, while his entire family stays at a bloody refuge for weeks on end!' I pointed out to them, almost shouting over their shoulders as they drove us home. I still felt high, the sense of achievement boosting my confidence and freeing my mind of one more thought of revenge.

When we arrived at Mum's, both policemen helped us empty

the car while the local children formed a rent-a-crowd scene beside us. 'Anytime you want to go back for stuff, just give us a call,' fair policeman assured me. 'I wouldn't risk going in alone, he's far too agitated and you'd just never get out again,' he said.

'So you're at your Mum's bit now?' the other one asked.

He'd remembered the house from the last commando raid we'd executed with Wanda and Frances.

'Aye, there's five of us crammed into a pensioner's cottage,' I was beginning to wheeze with the exertion of the last hour's activities. 'But you know something? It's just great to be free.'

Monday, 14 August

I wrote to John instructing him to demand a set of keys from Fatso. Maybe the thought of me going into his precious domain when he's out will make him think about selling up. He'd be so worried about me stealing some of his own stuff that it wouldn't be worth the heartache he's probably suffering even now. Anyway, despite my finding the episode extremely stressful, Mum and I felt good about his trembling, pathetic shamblings and truly saw a man near to breaking point. Some would say what a hard bitch I've become, and some would say that he deserves a damned site more hassle in his life, the bastard! He made such a fool of himself in front of those policemen. I can still see him charging about like a baby elephant behind me. I hope it makes him realise what I am prepared to do to get what I want. I know I am stronger than he is. I've coped with the past five years, I've managed to escape and with Mum's help I'll find another house and make a new life for me and the kids . . .

The following week saw us recovering after a day's excursion to Bathgate with all the kids. The phone rang and Mum jumped up to answer it, leaving me to listen to the one-sided conversation.

'Yes? Well, yes of course we would!' She sounded surprised and signalled the need of a pen to write something down onto the cover of the phone book. Another exchange I thought. We'd suffered two further let-downs since Mr Murray's cruel cliffhanger and I was becoming cynical about us ever finding a suitable exchange partner. 'That was the council asking us if we'd be interested in a five bedroomed house to rent in

Knightsridge!' she gasped. We jumped up, discovering enough instant energy to literally run towards the address the housing clerk had given us, calling the children from their play.

'What is it, Mum? Where are we going?' Ryan looked peeked and anxious with even Rosie recognising the note of urgency in her Nana's tone as she called her over. 'It's nothing bad,' I assured him but continued walking towards the address. Mum and I puzzled over the offer coming out of the blue as it had. Apart from my pathetic note of allotted points from West Lothian Council we'd had no indication of our position on any list and no suggestion that an offer was imminent from any of the housing clerks at the reception desk. However, here it was, a gift from fate and we raced excitedly towards the street entertaining images of the house we hoped to see.

The house and garden looked reasonable, but our hearts sank in unison when we saw the district in which it was situated. This was the rough part of town, where garden fences that had been kicked down stayed down and mafia-like children littered the streets and hung around a graffiti-stained shop that was only two doors away. It was like being deep in the heart of Beirut during its worst fighting and we knew we couldn't accept the tenancy. We trudged home dejectedly, still wondering how we could have received the offer in the first place and decided to go into the council offices the next morning.

Immaculate clerk sat proudly at her computer tapping out Mum's name efficiently. 'Two hundred and eighty-eight points,' she said, glancing up at us from the green screen.

'You're kidding!' Mum and I chorused in wonderment.

'Well . . . ' she squinted at the monitor, 'you are incredibly overcrowded, Mrs Stewart, and so you're practically at the top of the transfer list.'

We staggered home in contented silence, occasionally reminding each other of snippets of information the clerk had given us. What shocked me more was the fact that as a homeless person the council could only afford me 163 points, which meant approximately one year's wait before I got close to being offered anything.

I'd spent five miserable weeks in two refuges because it was deemed too risky to stay at Mum's address because of the overcrowding issue. Yet if I had gone directly there, we could have been housed before now because of the amount of points we would have gained on the transfer list.

Why hadn't any of the housing clerks mentioned this? We sat on the other side of their desk almost every week and they had both been fully informed of our situation, knowing how desperate we were. They knew that Mum was looking for an exchange yet they didn't advise her or me about our overcrowded status winning us enough points to get a larger house. And now we had been offered our first let, which we'd refused because of the bad district. That meant that we were one offer down with two to go before Mum's name was suspended from the transfer list for 12 months.

'Mark that area off your list of desirables, Mrs Stewart,' Immaculate clerk whispered wisely to Mum. 'Of course, the fewer areas you express an interest in the longer the wait,' she warned.

But we knew that the next offer could be soon, with another one after that if need be.

Tuesday, 5 September 1995
Today Mum and I traipsed about Livingston looking for empty houses. It pissed down on us. It was cold and lonely and when we got home, a nice lady from the Housing Department came to tell us about another house that was available to let!

This house is a bungalow in a newly renovated part of town and has four bedrooms and a shower-room, all well decorated. The garden is in an appalling state with broken fences all round and the odd smashed television set nestling amongst the knee-high grass. The next door house was empty and just as heavily boarded up as our one.

We don't know how bad this street is but the next one looks really rough. Once the local gangs notice there's no man around the household, they'll see us as an easy target. It happened in Pilton and Wester Hailes and I just don't think I could cope with that kind of hassle again. Could the boys get out to play without getting battered? Would Rosie be able to play in the garden without being spotted by someone's rabid Rottweiler sizing her up as an appetiser?

Mum was keen to accept this house, but she too had reservations about the area. The shower-room was extremely basic, with a sloping corked floor complete with drainage hole in the middle. A curtain rail did exist, but we certainly had no money to install a shower tray and the council were unwilling to help since they'd only just made it that way for the previous tenant who had been a wheelchair user. To refuse this offer meant that there was only one chance left. Anxiously she telephoned the housing clerk to refuse the house.

I attended my first counselling session at the health clinic feeling unenthusiastic about its merits in relieving the unbearable tension I felt. I introduced myself and we shook hands before she offered me a seat and it reminded me of past interviews I'd experienced. Annie, the counsellor, was a slim woman, a similar age to myself, and she appeared relaxed and informed about my reasons for attending.

I calmly began to detail the fantastic events of the past few months and before I realised it I was describing each event through floods of tears laced with the choicest expletives known to the English language. I roared and shouted, and questioned and bawled and yelled out my story in animated fashion while she sat primly before me nodding without comment and listening intently. I left her office with an appointment for the following week feeling as if an immense weight had been lifted from my chest. I'd said some terrible things, unrepeatable ramblings that I'd never consider saying to anyone who knew me. Just saying the words, without having someone judge my opinion, actually made me feel better and changed my attitude towards the art of counselling forever.

Sunday, 10 September 1995

Our lives rest on the next and final house offer. If it's in another bad district, we'll have to refuse and hope for an exchange. Nobody seems interested in exchanging with us. It's an unreal situation. We live day to day, waiting for the phone call, or the visit. Makes time go so slowly.

Rosie went off to meet her Daddy, happy and excited on Friday evening – only to return screaming, kicking and fighting, distressed and apparently exhausted. She *stood* beside the chair and fell asleep only 15 minutes after she got in. I suspect that Sam is allowing her to stay up later, which is understandable, but he must be missing out her daily nap and this is the third time she's returned in such a state. It'll look good for her to be crying and upset on her return to us of course. It smacks of 'I don't want to go back to Mummy's', and is particularly hurtful when I make the effort to sound enthusiastic about her going to stay at Daddy's. If he thinks he can use his two-year-old daughter to further his campaign he's sadly mistaken. As much as I'd like her to continue to see him, I'll go to court to lessen the residential access if I think she can't cope with it and what he's doing to her psychologically. I feel so much better after my session at the counsellor. Wish he could get the same help.

I still panic at the thought of meeting him and when I'm on the bus I'm terrified he'll get on at his stop but I'm getting stronger every day.

Slowly my sleeping and eating habits started to improve and I would doze until 9 a.m. whenever Rosie was away at her Dad's. Slight upsets and petty family crises didn't seem to signal the end of the world for me any more, and I had less time to dwell on my problems. I tried to concentrate on the boys, looking for positive ways to entertain them. I asked Annie about a counselling session for Ryan since Mum and I had noted his extreme agitation when it drew near to Sam's appearance at the house. He imagined the man still wanted to assault us and his mood would change the moment he realised Sam's presence was imminent.

'If he comes in here I'll belt him with this stick!' He brandished a knobbled branch he'd discovered in the woods with a determined frown on his face before being herded off towards the back bedroom to calm down.

I decided that in future I would deliver Rosie to Sam's address as this would mean less upset for the boys and they could exist without Sam encroaching on their playing space every fortnight. No doubt he would object to it at first as he objected to absolutely everything I requested through John. I despaired at the thought of his pettiness lasting throughout the next 14 years before Rosie was considered an adult. Sam continued to avoid any kind of conversation with me or Mum and totally ignored the boys if one of them accompanied me up to the house to collect their sister. Old neighbours saw me and stopped to chat.

They recoiled in horror when I told them I was homeless. They looked towards the house and Sam with complete disdain and tutted disgustedly at the law's tolerance of his resistance to selling.

Sometimes I felt embarrassed about my situation and tried to avoid meeting old acquaintances and neighbours whom Sam and I had known as a couple. I was worried about what some would say. Sam's educated speech and charming exterior fooled people into believing what a caring, sensible man he was. Even the policemen who had watched him pout and pick at my every move judged the man more by his authoritative manner and calm exterior.

I didn't try to convince anyone I knew about the humiliating silences, the terrifying rages of violence and controlling nature. They could just as well think that my confident and friendly attitude masked some sinister deed I'd committed during our relationship. What some would say was the main reason why I stayed silent. I looked back on some of the most hurtful and distressing incidents and wondered how I coped with it all. And now we were free – well, almost. He'd always be around for as long as he still wanted to see Rosie and that would be for the rest of his life, I hoped.

The future for me meant leading Ryan, David and possibly Rosie out of that period of our lives, with as little after-effect as possible. Mum and I were happy to be living together again. We always got on well, while realising the need for each other's personal space to be recognised and considered. Once we got a house, I could turn my thoughts to part-time work and higher education. Anything was possible now that I didn't have anyone sowing subtle seeds of doubt in my abilities.

What I had suffered at the hands of my controlling husband was far less than some women had endured. I never had bruises the size of dinner plates nor broken bones or any long-term effects from the physical effects of the abuse I received. I'd decided to leap into the great unknown that is life after such a relationship and the refuge was there to take us in.

In my opinion, what happened there was because of the combination of individuals living there at that particular point in time. If the workers had been a bit more attentive, if Debbie and Sonia had been a bit more responsible and less selfishly motivated in their actions and if I had reacted less impulsively things could have been different.

I carried negative baggage about men with the firmest grip and that would remain for a long time; possibly for the rest of my life. Everything seemed to hinge on our getting a house.

Presumably Sam would come to terms with the fact that we'd left him (he'd never admit to his behaviour being the cause of our flight, not even to himself) and begin to pick up his own life with a job and a girlfriend. He'd waste no time in ensnaring another gullible soul and I could practically write the script for the excuses he'd reel out to her in explanation of his plight.

He'd make her feel sorry for him, being all alone in that beautiful house without his family around. He'd sound so convincing, making sure not to admit to any part in the break-up of the marriage. No doubt he'd say I left for no particular reason, just like Linda had before me.

Maybe his new girlfriend will have children of her own from a previous relationship, and a house and a car and a job. Maybe she'll have the same kind of life that I had, just five years ago.

Thursday 14 September 1995
WE'VE GOT A HOUSE!!!!!!